AMAZON FBA

A Step By Step Guide To Building Your E-Commerce
Business And Find Your Passive Income Freedom.
A Model Approach For Beginners Who Want To Work At
Home And Selling Private Label Products.

Logan Brand

Table of contents

Introduction

Many people don't realize it: you can make money on Amazon! And we will show you how to do that on a big scale.

When we talk about big-scale, we talk about millions of dollars, like many Amazon FBA sellers are making. It will not be easy, but it will be worth it.

One important thing, the most important: you need to make sure that you have the right approach to get the sales, and to build up a great business. This means you need to read this book thoroughly before you make any actions.

If you don't understand something in this book, make sure to revisit it as much as possible, so you get a better idea.

We spent a lot of effort and time in providing you the best information possible, but if you don't put in the work, you will not see the results. We can give you all the information, but if you don't apply yourself, reading this book is likely to be just a waste of time.

Now, enough with the premises and let's start!

Chapter 1:

What is Amazon FBA?

If you haven't heard of Amazon by now, chances are you are living under a rock. Jeff Bezos, who is worth over $150 billion, found the company in the early 90s, as a storefront for books. Fast forward to now where Amazon is sells anything you could want, from toilet papers to full television set Amazon, has got you covered. How Amazon FBA works is simple. First, you find a product from a cheap supplier then you sell it to people at a markup price on Amazon leaving you with some profit in your pocket.

Now if you're wondering, what does the FBA stand for? It stands for "Fulfillment by Amazon". Think of Amazon as similar to Shopify, except for two things:

1. You will be selling your products on Amazon;
2. You will have to ship your products to their warehouse before you can start fulfilling orders.

So you will have to find a supplier and ship the products to the nearest Amazon warehouse, so the upfront investment would be a little bit higher as compared to Shopify. To break it down here is the approximate cost of startup:

- Buying products in bulk for cheap $1000 – $3000;
- If you sell more than 40+ items a month, you will have to pay $39.99;

On the lower end, you can get started for USD 1000 to USD 3000 plus $39.99 a month if you sell more than 40 products. There is also a charge per shipped product, but that will be decided upon your payout.

So even though there is a more significant upfront investment, there are still a lot of advantages, for instance, you will be promoting your product on a website that already gets a bunch of free traffic. Meaning that you will have more success, in the beginning, to sell your products as compared to other methods. Another great benefit would be that there is no need to worry, creating a storefront as Amazon would be your storefront.

So, without further ado, let's get into the specifics of starting your business from the scratch using Amazon FBA. Mostly you will have to figure out three things before you begin to advertise on this platform:

1. Profitable Product
2. Finding a supplier
3. Advertising

Profitable product

Now, to find a profitable product, you have to remember two things:

1. Find out what is selling on Amazon;
2. Check the competition on Amazon.

You need to make sure that there is a demand for the product and secondly, there is not a lot of competition for that product on Amazon as it can make it challenging to sell it online. So making sure that these two things are in check, it is imperative for you to the success on this platform. And, also remember that finding a profitable product depends on uniqueness.

Let's take the fidget spinner, for example, although unique it offered its users something to fidget with hence "fidget spinner". It helped people to get rid of any "fidgety" feeling they might have so to speak and also is a fun little game for the children, so although it isn't necessary to find a product like a fidget spinner it is essential to dive into a profitable niche.

To find a profitable niche, there are a couple of ways to do so, and one of them using Amazon. So for some that might know, Amazon is the biggest e-commerce website of this day and age, meaning whatever sells on Amazon will most likely sell anywhere in the world.

So to find a profitable product or niche could be very easy on Amazon, the first thing you would want to do is check the best sellers list on Amazon. This will give you a guide of what is selling online right now, the second check to see how many niche specific products are for sale online.

10

So if you check the best sellers list and you see five examples of an iPhone case on there, the chances are that iPhone and electronics accessories is a great niche to get into.

One thing to remember, though, most of the products on the best sellers list already have a competitive price, which would be hard for beginners to beat.

So what you want to do is find a sub-niche in that category, for instance, you have decided to use the electronic accessories as your niche. What you will do is find a "keyword" or a slot that has more than 6 products in the top 100,000 best sellers list on Amazon and has less than 1,000 results.

If you look up "iPhone phone case glitter" as your keyword and if you check to see the top 6 products are rated at 100,000 on the best sellers list, and the results are less than a 1,000, then this would be a great product and a niche to get into.

Since everything is getting so competitive these days online, it is essential to find these super-niche products if you want to be successful from the get-go in this business.

Thus making sure you see this super-niche on Amazon is recommended before you go ahead and invest your money on a product that may or may not sell. So, if you want to save your money and instead earn more money then do your research and find those "sub-niche" as there is a lot of money to be made there and just like always do your research.

Finding a supplier

Finding a supplier for your Amazon FBA business is quite easy as compared to Shopify, there are three ways of finding your supplier for Amazon in:

1. AliExpress;
2. Warehouse;
3. Big sales.

As you can see you have a lot of options as to where you could find your products. So, let's talk about each method.

Most suppliers use such websites like AliExpress as it can help you make money online without any troubles. The beauty of AliExpress is that it has about 99.9% of the things you want to sell or own, they have it and for a bargain of a price. So, it is a shame not to use these websites to find products and to resell it at a markup on Amazon.

Most of the products on AliExpress aren't of the highest quality. To find a product that would sell and help you make money for a long time, there are a couple of things you can to ensure: that you are not robbed of your investment. All you need to do is find the right supplier. To find the right supplier here is two things to check for:

1. The first thing is review's check the sellers' review on AliExpress: if the review is below a 4.5 out of 5 then chances are the seller is not reliable or has excellent quality products hence needs to be discarded from your supplier list.

2. The second thing to take note of would be to see how many orders the supplier has fulfilled. If a supplier has fulfilled more than 500 orders, then there is a high chance that the supplier is reliable and has excellent quality products. So, if these two things check out, then you can start to order from them.

Warehouse

Using warehouses nearby you to find cheap supplies for your product can be a great alternative compared to using the traditional way of Ali-express. Now, most people use places like *Costco.com* to find cheap supplies in bulk and sell them off on Amazon.

So, for you to find a warehouse can be a great option as it can save you the shipping cost and you can also check out the product in person before you decide to purchase it.

Now, there are some pros and cons to this method of finding supplies. The first one would be the fact that it is hard to find great warehouses or great product supplies using this method. Even though Costco is used by some people in their Amazon for business, it still has some flaws like the way it is packaged. Sometimes Costco packages the product in such a manner that it is hard to resell it. But, if you do find products in Costco to resell then do it! These products will yield you a lot of profits.

The second problem using this method would be to find warehouses that sell your products. Here is the thing: finding a warehouse that sells your products besides Costco can be a challenge when you first start on Amazon.

14

So, if you do find a warehouse which does sell the products that you are looking for, then chances are it would be a cheaper option as compared to Ali express. Ideally, if you can use other warehouses in your county to find products, as it can be a more affordable option.

Finally, I would like to talk about utilizing big sales which can be used to find products which you can resell, utilizing Black Friday, Cyber Monday, to save money on the products that you want or need. Luckily, you can use these sales to bulk up on your products which you can sell later on Amazon at a low price.

For example, a product that would cost you around $75 on Amazon would be going for $35 on that specific day. So what you can do is buy the product in bulk at the price of $35 and then wait a couple of weeks and sell it on Amazon for $65 undercutting your competition, which would mean more sales for you!

But, the problem with this method is that it isn't as recurring as the other two methods. Although it can be used as a great tool, it is indeed short-lived so capitalize on it as much as you can.

Hopefully, this helped you figure out how to find the right supplier for your product and business. Just remember that either of these three methods would work, just make sure that you are doing everything in your power to save money on the supplies, so make sure to pick the cheapest supplier every time you have to restock your inventory.

E-commerce vs Amazon FBA

As you know, Amazon FBA is very similar to dropshipping and e-commerce except there is one big difference.

The difference is that you will be marketing your products on the biggest retailer online. Now, this could be positive and also negative.

The other positives, behind this, are that you have access to billions of visitors every day, which means that you don't have to advertise to get visitors. If you have your keywords written correctly then you will get free traffic alongside free sales. Whereas in the e-commerce world, you would have to spend money on getting traffic.

The other positive behind amazon would be the brand awareness, many people feel extremely comfortable buying from Amazon, on the other hand, it is very hard to get people to trust your site when you have your store. That being said, there are some negatives.

One of the negatives would be that there is more competition on Amazon as there will be many more people just like you looking to sell products online.

Another negative with Amazon would be that it is very hard to start if you have no money. When dropshipping you can easily ship a single product once someone places an order.

With Amazon, you will have to invest and buy the product in bulk. In most cases, this would work out and make you money. But sometimes, it could lead to your product sitting and collecting dust. Overall, after looking at the positives and negatives Amazon FBA can yield your Amazon cash flow if done correctly. We will teach you how it's done and, by the end of the book, you will have all the tools you need in order to be successful.

Advertising

Now to make sure everyone is on the same page, even though Amazon offers us such a fantastic source of free traffic. It is still recommended to invest in some paid traffic. You have to take into consideration the fact that Amazon has so many products for sale on its website that sometimes it just becomes hard to showcase every single product on sale to people.

So to get some sales on your Amazon FBA account you might have to invest in some paid advertising, now there are two methods you can use to advertise your products.

The first one would be to utilize Amazon's in-built tool to start marketing, the second one would be to use YouTube to announce your product.

So to begin with we will talk about using Amazon's in-built advertising tool, it is quite simple to use and effective, look up keywords related to your product and start advertising accordingly. Then you set up a daily budget similar to Facebook's way of advertising, and there you have your Amazon advertising.

The second one can be done for free, but there is a trick involved. Now, most of the YouTubers use Amazon's very own affiliate marketing program to make money.

What you can do is ask them to promote your products on YouTube which would help them earn some affiliate commission and make you some money.

Finally, you can use Facebook's paid advertising platform for advertising your very own products.

How much money can you make?

So, of course, everyone wants to know how much money they can make. Well to begin with I would like to say a lot! Yes, you can make a lot of money doing this business model. But there is a catch if you want to make loads of money this business can't be passive in the beginning.

There will be a lot of trials and errors before you can indeed make this business passive. Now the good part is that once you get the ball rolling, it takes little to no effort to upkeep the company. So if you follow everything written in this book correctly, you can make anywhere from $1,000 to $100,000.

Now I did say a lot of money, not infinite money, unlike Shopify there is a cap on the income. Unfortunately, you can't expect to make more than 2 million a year from this business model just because it isn't a brand you created so to grow it even farther than that could be a task.

So, if you want to become a millionaire, you technically can and if you're going to make an extra $1,000 a month you most definitely work as it is entirely up to you to decide. Either way, there is some hard work needed in the beginning to start earning money.

To conclude this chapter, I would like to remind you of a couple of things before you get started on your Amazon business. Remember that it takes time and effort to begin this business, but once you get the ball rolling, you can make infinite amounts of money with it.

Remember that for you, to make money in this business you need to find the right supplier who will help you with delivering high-quality products to your clients.

Secondly, you will have to make sure that you adverse your product the right way by utilizing paid advertising tools provided. But the main thing to worry about is to make sure that you indeed have a winning product. Remember it takes time and effort to find a winning product, and with the information provided in this book, you can find one.

So keep trying, and eventually, it will materialize into the business that you are looking for. This chapter is to give you an overview of Amazon FBA.

Chapter 2:
Which product to sell?

Selling on Amazon needs an entrepreneurship skill which could take some risks, just like any other business out there. Taking calculated risks requires a complete understanding of what you're doing, being extra careful, and knowing what to avoid. Like in any selling business, your sales inflow depends on the products that you have and most importantly, it should be products that sell.

Otherwise, your inventory will be non-productive and will not make money for you. It is expected that there would be challenges when choosing a good product to sell; that's why this chapter will tackle the preparation to choose a good product. Don't have a product to sell on Amazon yet? Practically, you can sell almost ANYTHING and EVERYTHING on Amazon!

You don't need to manufacture products to sell. You can list products from more than 20 product categories and the "Everything Else" category is one of that. These are the items that do not match any existing categories. You can start selling on Amazon with any product you can think of. But, just like any other program, certain items need approval from Amazon before you can list in any product category.

Can you imagine selling items from the thrift stores? The items found in thrift stores are one of the popular types of items to sell on Amazon. You can also start listing some clearance items like media items, health and beauty items, or toys and board games. With Amazon FBA, buying a low-cost inventory in tiny quantities is a potential money-making business.

What to Sell?

Having a good product to sell is the most important part of the business to make real money. As an online seller, opportunities come from the products you sell. As I talk about "products," I mean finding a "profitable product" to sell.

I'm not pertaining to a product niche, which you will focus on. But why not find a product niche? Well, looking for a certain type of product can overwhelm you with too much product information, which is unnecessary and irrelevant as you start your selling business.

Trust me, looking for a product niche will not bring you to finding the right one unless you want to branch out or create a brand. The thing that you should care about most is having that "single profitable product" to sell and get a good product for your online selling business.

Find the perfect product

Deciding what products to sell can be difficult, so to get you prepared for getting a good product, here are my criteria of what a good product is:

1. Small and light product

Definitely, the size and weight of your product matters in determining a good product to sell, especially when shipping is concerned. The lighter and smaller the product is, the cheaper it is to ship.

Especially, if you will be dealing with customers globally. You don't need to sell products like furniture or kitchen appliances. Think of a product that can be delivered easily.

2. Consistent and non-seasonal

Taking advantage of the season when customers rush into shopping seems to be a good opportunity, but it's not advisable to focus on such products. It would only leave you tons of leftover inventories after the season. A good product is timeless, which maintains a consistent stream of buyers all year round.

3. The price range of $10-$200

You can try to start with products from this range and though it may take you a lot of capital, it's worth a try. Margin from this price range is fair enough to give you a profit. I also must say that products at a higher price than this are much riskier.

4. Sold at 100% markup

This is one criterion that I think will greatly benefit you. If you can sell a product twice the price you purchased, then it gives you a 50% margin. Isn't it a good product to sell? You doubled its price, so your effort to find that product will be an outstanding achievement.

5. Fair seller volume

Competition is part of any business, but there are still other products untapped by most sellers. The point is not to sell a product that has many sellers who already sell thousands of units a month. A product with little competition should not be discouraging at all; try to have a product that has a fair number of sellers to compete with.

6. Non-essential item

It is advisable not to sell what you buy and use such as foods, clothes, and other essentials. You'll end up competing in basic product markets while the non-essential items remain untapped. It only needs to determine the target market to identify a profitable non-essential item to sell. Don't sell potatoes, but potato baskets. Don't sell bottled water, but stylish reusable drinking straws. You get the idea.

7. Specific product

A good product to sell should address a specific need of buyers. For example, earrings or dangled earrings seem to be an interesting product. There are many designs of dangled earrings, and so, you can look for a specific design like "lightweight multi-leaf dangle earrings" to list on Amazon.

8. Non-mechanical item

Selling pieces of machinery like hydraulic lifts and saws can only give you headaches. Good products are those that are non-mechanical because it does not demand high quality and great warranties as compared to mechanical products.

9. Durable product

These products do not require "perfect" shipping practices to avoid breakage. If products are fragile, there will always be a possibility of delivering your item into parts and pieces, which can cause trouble for you and your customers. As the seller, you are ultimately responsible for the customer's experience with the product, and the durability of the product makes a good and lasting impression.

10.   Products without a trademark

Some laws prohibit others from selling trademarked products. Considering the restrictions and regulations of selling, a certain product is like having a less manageable item. A good product to sell will not lead you to be sued afterward. Counterfeit products should be avoided as well.

11.   Product serving passion or pain

Products that sell best are those that serve passion, solve a problem, or relieve the pain for buyers. Many customers are actively seeking a solution to their needs rather than discovering a new product. Always consider that a good product should have an ultimate purpose for your customers.

12.   Consumable or disposable item

Once you have loyal customers, selling to existing customers becomes easier than new ones. Get a product that is replaceable after the customer gets the most out of the product for a certain period. Good products may not need to have a short lifespan or to be perishable items.

13.   Scalable product

Thinking of the future is a considerable move at the start of the business. Is your product scalable if your business takes off? Without knowing what the future would be, getting ready for possible growth, sales start with having a good product that can cope up with possible high demand. The factors that may affect the scalability are materials and sources of your products. Are the materials difficult to find, or will there be enough suppliers if orders increase in number? Try to answer these questions when you see a potential product to sell.

14.   Products with a growing market

You must understand where your product falls. The product should stand at a growing market. Products may fall as fad or trend rather than into a stable or growing market. You can profit from each market, but there is a long-term opportunity for products in a growing market.

There's no such thing as a perfect product but what matters is minimizing the risks in choosing a product to sell.

The product must be well thought and strategically researched. Various factors are considered, such as price, marketability, profitability, competition, as well as the physical condition of the product.

You must realize that the ultimate foundation of online selling is choosing profitable products to sell. This decision is critical to business operations because selling online is not merely getting the products that interest you or having a product that you can produce. You must sell products that buyers need and are interested in.

Amazon Product Restrictions

It is also important to keep in mind. So, you won't waste your time scouting for products, and later on, discover that Amazon won't approve your listing.

Here's the list of product requirements and restrictions you should be aware of:

- **Categories for approval**

  Know the checklist that will guide you on how to list products from inappropriate product categories. Currently, there are 24 categories that have requirements for listing products (e.g., beauty, clothing & accessories, collectibles, jewelry, sports collectibles).

- **Labeling of date and temperature-sensitive products**

  Know how to prepare products with expiration dates both for human and animal products (e.g. ingestible and consumable products).

- **Restricted Products**

  You should be guided by the laws and regulations of the product you will sell. Any illegal and unsafe products are prohibited, and if you have listed such products, your Amazon account may be suspended or terminated, without reimbursing any unfulfilled inventory.

- **FBA will not process hazardous materials and dangerous items**

  Any product that belongs to this category (e.g., explosives, aerosols, poisons, vehicle tires).

Determining which product is good and permitted requires a guide to make a wise decision.

Review these criteria whenever you have products in mind. It will prepare you to have a profitable product listing, especially when you researched them well.

Choosing the right products to sell could be overwhelming. Go over this chapter for the guidelines on how to look for potential products to sell. These references will give you information about at which marketplace to look for a product to sell online, the number of competitors, and the right prices to sell.

Online Wholesale Product Sources

Here is the list of online sites to help you research on good products to sell.

Etsy

This is a relatively untapped venue for buying and selling mostly handmade, vintage, and other products.

eBay

Get an idea of what products are selling, its volume, and price from this site. When searching for products, filter the prices and the selling frequency by checking the "Completed Listings" button.

Amazon

One of the best sites you can research on to find good products; the same online retail site that you will sell your product. Use the Amazon Best Seller Rank as a tool to find a good product.

Alibaba

This is the leading platform for global wholesale trade. It is a venue that helps you find overseas suppliers of your product listing and is used to check prices. Make sure to check the "Gold Supplier" button when searching for products and suppliers. It will filter according to quality suppliers and those that are scammers.

Barn Cat Mercantile

Visit this site if you're looking for a wholesale price of wax-dipped LED candles in the US and Canada. Get the wholesale price by providing them your store information.

Enrico Products

If you're looking for eco-friendly kitchen products and gadgets, check out this site. This is a site where you can register as a Retailer and be able to access the full complement of resources, including catalogs, photos, sales materials, and promotions. Avail also the products with wholesale prices from their system. 4Black Paws - For the dog lover market this site offers cute designer dog collars. This could be one of the products you may find to be a good one.

WholesaleCrafts.com

This is a source of handmade and craft products that offers an online marketplace for buyers and artists, which you can recheck online. Serenity Tea Sips - Another online marketplace that offers a line of loose-leaf teas and tisanes. Browse their products and see if you can resell any of them.

Snowonder

This is an online shopping site that sells instant artificial snow with various packages. Be sure to take note of all the details about this product and how you can handle it if you choose to list it as your product.

Shiny Extras

Looking for fashion jewelry items? Check out this site, which manufactures offer to choose for high-quality Swarovski Crystal products like earrings, bracelets, necklaces, and rings.

Design

This is an online shopping site for trendy totes and aprons, all made in the USA. Check their fun designs and other products like fan gear, sorority gifts, and accessories.

ANMEZ

For innovative products, this site offers a product called Greentest, a food safety-testing device. This product detects if fruits and vegetables are cultivated improperly and helps people make a healthier decision about their food by evaluating the concentration of nitrates.

AT Imports Ltd

A one-stop one shop wholesale warehouse that originally offers Amish iron and woodcraft products. Currently, the store has a vast quantity of products, from craft supplies to seasonal items, floral and home décor. You can register online and be a member by including your tax ID, Resale tax licenses or Business License number and you'll be able to access their catalog.

Santa Fe Stoneworks

This online store has beautiful custom knives and cutlery products. There are various knife collections to choose from, all handles are one-sided, though it can be specified to be double-sided with additional markup.

The GlideHanger

This is a site of clothing hanger for narrow-necked garments that makes it functional for all types of clothes. If you find this item fits your criteria, contact the customer service for product details.

Station 1 Wholesale

An online store that offers unusual gifts and home decors at wholesale price with new products weekly. Find a product from the list of gifts like tin signs, kitchen, garden décor, Jim Shore feature, vases, clocks, and more other gift items.

Outdoor Active Gear

Check out this site that supplies products like coolers, camouflage, and different outdoor activity gears. These are just a few of the online stores available on the web.

Research from these sites and look at the market data to have a comparison between Alibaba and the rest of the online retailer sites.

As you go along, you'll gain opportunities from several venues for finding a good product.

Just remember the criteria of a good product when you do the research. The data you get from these sites can be listed on a spreadsheet to make a summary and track the different products you'll find.

You can check a sample spreadsheet which is advisable to do from Will Mitchell, a serial entrepreneur. Get the markup estimate of each product you'll find, especially if a product fits all the criteria of a good product.

Go over your list as you calculate the selling price of a product.

Honestly, there's no fixed process in researching a good product. But, there are several ideas that you can try to come up with products by using a search such as:

- Products that have been trending in recent years;
- Random objects around;
- People buy consistently with little impulse;
- Products from random search results Randomly clicking the online retail sites (Amazon, eBay, Etsy);
- Researching may take you less than half an hour to find a product.

Remember to look for specific products by going through each product subcategories you're searching for. Try to list a few products on your spreadsheet. Afterward, recheck each product and make a comparison. Make sure to double-check and review according to the criteria so you'll avoid having a bad product on your list.

Offline Wholesale Product Sources

Take your time to find a good product because the core of your business and your success lies in the products you'll list and sell.

You have to think and decide which products will be profitable and you can work on for years. Sometimes you can also source some products with your regular household shopping, social outings, and other fun activities. Surely, you'd love doing your business, especially when done as if you're not working. Here are some offline wholesale product sources where you can find a good product:

Garage Sale

Most sellers start their inventory from home or garage sales because it opens great opportunities to make huge profits on inventory- turning 100-1000% profit. There are varieties of products from garage sales that are cheap, and you can sell online for a higher price. To source from garage sales, select a few areas that you're interested in visiting or check the newspaper for some information on upcoming garage sales. Make sure always to start early when scouting items in garage sales to make sure that you'll get the best deal early on.

Thrift Stores

Sourcing items from thrift stores is a practical choice especially for sellers with a limited amount of capital to put up the inventory.

Looking for items in thrift stores does not mean looking for junk. You can find some new items and be able to sell them for big profits. You can also consider buying some used items at thrift stores and still profit from it.

You have the advantage of selling items from thrift stores because you'll have minimal competition from other sellers aside from the very high profits you can make from these items.

Just ensure that price stickers are removed and items are cleaned up before shipping via Amazon.

Manufacturers / Distributors

When sourcing products, another option to look into are manufacturers or distributors for wholesale orders.

They offer products with a small minimum order as you start your relationship with them and you can easily re-order an item that sells more. And, if the relationship with them prospers, you may ask for exclusivity to sell on Amazon. More so, different products can be tied up from these sources and come up with your packages and make a unique product.

On the other hand, finding wholesale sources may take some time to research and may not bring high margins. On your journey to selling on Amazon, you'll become an expert in finding a good product sooner or later. Expertise also comes as you continue to get familiar with the line of products you're listing, so you can better serve the needs of the customers.

Chapter 3:
Which niche to pick?

This is one of the most important steps, if not the most important step in the whole process of building your FBA business.

Niche selection involves picking products to sell that meet several certain criteria which I will share with you. Although niche selection can involve some elements of financial risk, I will only be recommending that you get into a niche that is suitable for your budget. I currently invest more than the average person getting started, but this is because I have built my business up from a point in which my budget was significantly smaller.

You do not need to invest more than you are financially comfortable with. Most importantly, if you carefully follow the steps in this section, any financial risk will be 99% safeguarded.

I strongly recommend that you are meticulous and really take your time on this section. Do not rush because this will be the main component in determining your final success. Follow the steps exactly as they are outlined. Try not to get hung up, be confident in knowing a niche is viable when you have done the necessary criteria research.

Categories not to sell

Firstly, I want to introduce you to the product categories that I strongly recommend you to avoid selling. Although it is possible to make a profit in these niches, generally it is very difficult to succeed in them. Therefore it is not a good place to start to get your business on the right track.

One of the factors that make some niches difficult to compete in is that they have strict requirements that must be met. For example, some niches require the seller to submit heaps of extra documentation, information, insurance articles, etc.

This involves a lot of back and forth with Amazon which will really stall your progress and will delay the time it takes for you to start selling.

As a guideline for you to follow, here is a list of product categories that I do not recommend you get into as your first niche:

- Automotive & Power Sports Clothing;
- Accessories & Luggage Collectible;
- Books Entertainment Collectibles;
- Gift Cards;
- Industrial & Scientific Jewelry;
- Shoes, Handbags & Sunglasses;
- Sports Collectibles;
- Toys & Games (requiring approval);
- Watches.

In addition to these, here are some other product categories that don't work well with the profitable system that I will be teaching you:

- All Book Categories;
- All Movies, Music & Game Categories;
- Software.

The reason why I really want to highlight these is that they have typically had very little success with myself and the majority of people that I have worked with. With all that said, you might want to experiment in these niches later on once you are more experienced and have already had a strong level of success. Although this might sound fairly restrictive, there are endless other categories and subcategories to choose from that are excellent to get into as a first niche.

And in the next subsection, I'll be showing you how to start the product brainstorming process to come up with viable and profitable niches.

Brainstorming

So you might be wondering: how do I start coming up with good product ideas? And the answer to this starts by asking yourself two simple questions... What are you interested in and passionate about?

As a start, I recommend that you think about what you are personally interested in, along with any hobbies and/or products that you are passionate about. Go ahead and write down all of your ideas.

The reason I suggest this is that if you are already interested and passionate about something, you are likely to already know a great deal about it.

You will have some level of expertise in this area which can ultimately give you a competitive advantage. Another reason is that if these products turn out to be best sellers when you do your further research in Amazon, then this will be an ideal niche for you. You will have an infinite amount of motivation for your product. One final benefit is that by using your existing knowledge, you will be likely to discover areas in which you can improve the product for the end-user.

Again, giving you that extra competitive advantage! Remember even if your interest isn't directly related to a product, try to think of any tools, equipment, parts, etc. that are related. These could be viable niches.

What do you buy? The second key question is to ask yourself what you have personally bought in the last 30-90 days?

An easy way to discover this is to look at your credit card statements. Does anything, in particular, stand out that you have bought online?

If so, go ahead and write these down. Another option is to go out and ask friends/family what they have bought online recently. This will give you even more product ideas to add to your list.

Bestsellers

The most effective way to start finding profitable niches is to look at the best sellers in each category and sub-category. Many of these products can regularly be doing sales volumes of as high as $20,000 or more a day!

If you come across any bestsellers, take these as ideas and write these down. I will later be showing you how you can work out exactly how well products are selling by using Amazon's sales ranking system. I always tell people to make sure that they enjoy this process!

Have fun, be creative with your thinking, and in the next section, we will be going into detail about how you can narrow your product ideas down to 5 viable niches.

Competition levels

At this point, you should have some product ideas as a result of the brainstorming methods. Now it's time to start looking at Amazon to discover the competition levels within a niche.

When getting into selling on Amazon, you can go for a niche with low levels of competition and dominate that niche, or you can go for a competitive niche with a higher sales volume.

I actually recommend going into a niche with higher levels of competition because a low competition niche will more often than not have a low sales volume and very sporadic sales. There is usually a reason why a niche has low levels of competition!

You want to be making consistent sales and profit each and every day, and high competition niches have more people searching for products, meaning there are many more chances to make sales. Even though there are more sellers to compete with, there are a number of tools and tactics to stand out from the competition that I will be teaching you.

With that said, you don't want to get into a niche that is overly competitive and saturated. This can lead to very high costs in advertising and other methods you will need to use to stand out.

I will now show how to find a niche with higher competition levels, but still enough room for you to get in and start making sales from competitors. The best way to gauge competition in a niche is to simply look at the number of reviews for the top products within that niche. If the top 5-10 products in a niche have a large number of reviews, this niche may be too competitive.

Also, make sure to check the best sellers rank. If the top five products are bellow 50,000 bsr then it is a great product to start selling.

Amazon

As we know by now, Amazon is the biggest online store at the moment. It means that whatever sells on Amazon sells anywhere. So, if your goal is to find a niche that will make you money and is profitable then you need to review Amazon's products.

If you have visited Amazon's website to purchase a product or anything of that matter, bellow you will see the best sellers rank under the product description. What that bestseller rank symbolizes is how much the product is being bought, this is very important for you to note. If the product is not selling on Amazon, which is the biggest e-commerce store in the world, it will not sell anywhere. Now here is what you are going to do in order to find a product that sells.

The very first thing you are going to do is get on your computer and go to Amazon's website. Now, I want you to do it and go on to the best sellers page on Amazon. This page will give you a rough idea of what sells and what doesn't, and also will show you the niche products which are selling already.

Anything on Amazon's best sellers page will most likely sell, that is if you can offer it at a cheaper price. Regardless of which platform you will be using for your drop-shipping business if Amazon has the same product for sale as you do it will have it for the same price or cheaper than you would. This is the case most of the time, but If you can sell it for cheaper than your competitors on Amazon then you have a winning product! Congrats.

Now if that's not the case, it is out time to find an untapped niche. So go to the best sellers page on Amazon and look at the top 100 on that list carefully, if you see similar products from the same niche then this niche is profitable. But it could be hard to penetrate into that specific market or niche, this is where we find a micro-niche. For example, if the niche is "iPhone accessories" and there are multiple iPhone accessories on the bestseller list, what we will do is search up iPhone accessories in the Amazon search bar.

Then we will go through the top six products and check to see their best sellers list. If the bestseller list showcases a number below 50,000 for all six items at the top, then this niche is profitable.

Hypothetically, you can sell in this niche and make some great profits. But if the competition is high then there are fewer chances of you actually making profits. So, if you want to make sure the completion is low, look at the search engine number.

If the search engine number has a number lower than 5,000 items, then the niche is small and if the top six products have a ranking of lower than 50,000 on the best sellers rank then you have a winning product and a niche to get into. For instance, if you search up "iPhone accessories" and it has 20,000 items for sale, it would be harder for you go into. On the other hand, if you search up iPhone phone cases and it has lower than 5,000 items for sale and the top six items best seller rank is lower than 50,000, you have a winner at hand. So, this is how you use Amazon to find a profitable niche.

Shopify Stores and eBay

The second method for you is going to be examining online websites and stores to figure out which product is selling.

One of the best ways to find out which product sells and which one does not is look at all the dropshipping websites out there and simply studying them. For finding out Shopify stores, go on a website https://myip.ms/ or simply google that term.

What this website allows you to do, is look at all the top Shopify stores which are getting the most traffic and perhaps the most amount of orders out there. Many successful Shopify dropshippers tend to utilize this website and to study for them in order to grow their own business.

Now the first thing you should be doing is to go on this website and look at all the top hundred pages on it. What you should be looking at are the products they are selling and how they are making the websites look to allow them to convert a lot better.

This is one of the best tools you can use to figure out what you should be selling in your niche, as a lot of niches doing very well in regards to sale in traffic. Make sure you learn from these websites and utilize it at the unlimited possibility. Similar to the way you would find products on Amazon, this will allow you to find out which websites are actually selling and how they're selling a product.

Overall allow yourself to have a better Shopify store and hints at selling more products overall. Whenever you have time go on this website, sit down and look at all the top hundred pages and really learn from them. Looking at successful websites is one of the best ways to find out which products are selling and a Shopify dropshipping store theme.

Now that we have talked about Shopify and how to figure out which products are selling on Shopify let's talk about eBay and how you can learn from selling on eBay which can both translate on Shopify and eBay stores.

When you go on eBay, you need to look at the top searches of what products come up.

Most of the time websites will show you the products which are selling really good on top. As you know, eBay is one of the biggest websites where you buy products at a really good deal.

Once you found a product on eBay, with a really good price side on it and it showed up on top that should be one of your cues to show you that products are selling very good on eBay which will mean, it will sell really good on Shopify and eBay store.

Another way to find out if products are selling on eBay is to look up your niche. For example, if your niche is "camping or outdoors", simply type "outdoors" on the eBay search engine and look at the top 5 products that show up. Most of the time those top 5 products, are selling very good on eBay which means they will sell very good if you try and sell it on eBay at a lower price, or if you open up your own Shopify store and start dropshipping it.

Make sure whatever you do to figure out if you can find the products which are selling on eBay and other Shopify stores at a very reasonable price where you can sell it for cheaper.

If you can sell the product for a lower price than your competitors, such as Shopify stores on eBay, are not be able to scale up your business.

Sure, products are selling on eBay and on Shopify, but it is no use if you can't find it at a lower price so keep that in mind when you're looking at other stuff and finding out products for your niche.

One other way to find out that products are profitable or are selling very good in your niche is to look it up on

Google. For example, if you're in the automotive car niche and you want to sell something simply look up car automotive in Google search and the first thing that pops up which is selling a product.

The chances are that website makes good money selling it, and so can you if you manage to find a cheaper link to your product. Many dropshippers have found amazing products simply by looking it up on Google, and it is a straightforward yet effective method to find out about good products.

One of the main ways that you can find out about profitable products, use all these techniques to ensure that you are in the right position to be selling products and making the most money out of them.

Just remember that finding the right product might not just happen easily, if you do this research, you need time and energy to actually find a winning product.

The first couple of times you might try and find a winning product, but even if you did all the research right it might not work out for you.

However, if you keep going at it and not give up, you will find the part that you're looking for an overall sold more units of it. Take the game of dropshipping and starting your own business as trial and error. You will fail, eventually but if you keep going you will build a beautiful business for yourself and start making the money which you have been looking for. All you have to do is be patient and give it some time.

Does anyone remember the fidget spinner? It came out a couple of years ago and it was really famous, as you can imagine it made a lot of money for the people who created it and to anyone who sold it. Whoever sold the product when it was at its peak made a whole lot of money. People were buying this product like it was water it truly became a necessity. It was wild!

You can see fidget spinner as an example of a highly profitable product and from the title, you might have guessed it.

Yes, we are going to be talking about highly profitable products and how to find them. Now, here's the good news, finding a profitable product is easy, but to sell it at the right place and the right time is when it gets a bit tricky. Before going ahead I want to tell you what a product is and the different types of products.

So, a product is something you trade or give someone for money.

Now there are two types of products, the first one is a commodity product and the second one would be considered a niche product.

A commodity product would be something every human needs for survival, a couple of examples would be bread, water, car, etc. These products are needed by most people so they can survive or sustain a certain lifestyle, which means they will do whatever it takes to get these products to survive.

Now the other product is a niche-based product, a niche product would be something people don't buy it out of necessity rather they buy it because they like it. An example of these products would be dog bracelets. So by no means, you would need these products for survival but there is defiantly a need for it.

Ideally, we would all like to sell in the commodity niche as there is a constant demand for it. But to sell things in the commodity would be a bit challenging since the people who are at the top of the food chain have spent so much money on the commodity products that in order for you to sell and actually make good money you will have to spend a lot of money on advertisement.

Now getting into a niche product can work and could make you money, but even though there is less competition it could be hard to get into.

Remember the fidget spinner I was talking about earlier? What kind of product do you think it is? Commodity or a niche product?

If your answer was niche then you are completely wrong: a fidget spinner was a combination of both commodity and a niche product. The fidget spinner was a product that was made for people who need something to fidget with, and through advertising and popularity became a commodity.

Do you see where I am going with this? If you want to find a winning product, find one which is both: a commodity product and a niche based product.

Chapter 4:
How to create your account?

This is it! Start your selling business by signing up with Amazon.

Amazon.com is the marketplace for selling your products around the globe, and everything begins by creating a seller account on Amazon.

Whether as an individual or professional, you have easy access to Amazon that enables fast-selling online. Get started to sell on Amazon with no need of having your own website! Just do a self-registration process at Amazon Services Seller Central site, without talking to any salesperson. Before I give you a step-by-step guide on how to create your Amazon seller account, here is a list that you'll need particularly for a Professional Seller account:

- Business name, address and contact information;
- Credit card with valid billing address which is internationally chargeable;
- Phone number (you'll be reached here during the registration);
- Tax identity information.

Amazon seller types

As mentioned, when you sign-up with Amazon, you have to select which seller account type you prefer, either Professional or Individual. Each account type has a corresponding plan and features.

To help you decide on which account plan to create, here is the comparison of the two plans:

1. Individual Seller

With an Individual plan, a seller is spared from monthly selling fees except for the commission that Amazon gets from each item sold. This option is usually for sellers who plan to sell less than 40 products a month. If at the start, your budget is insufficient or you want to start slow and build your inventory cautiously, you may opt to register as an individual seller. You will only be charged for every successful order. You may always upgrade to Professional, if necessary.

2. Professional Seller

The Professional plan is based on a monthly fee. It is suitable for sellers who plan to sell an unlimited number of products. Sellers are also allowed to list products not currently being sold on Amazon. This option is usually chosen by sellers who own offline stores and can sell more than 40 products a month. If you prefer to have more features, then go for the Professional account. Don't worry if you change your mind later. You can always switch from Professional to Individual account. Just change this from your account settings and all the features will be changed to an Individual account. You have to consider that registering as a Professional seller, the monthly subscription is charged upon completion of registration, and so considering your finances is important. But, if there are current promotional offers, you may want to consider getting the offer. I advise that at the start of your registration you get to know the other fees which will be charged when an item is sold. This is also very important to review when calculating how much product you will sell.

How to set-up an Amazon Seller Account

Here's a guide to set-up your seller account on Amazon:

Step 1

Make sure you have decided which seller type you want to register when you open your browser to this site:

http://services.amazon.com/content/sell-on-amazon.htm

If you're not from the US and want to register locally, check the flag/country choices at the right upper corner of the page to ensure that you will be registering at the local Amazon site. It will redirect you to a local Amazon site.

Step 2

Select the seller account type by clicking the corresponding button, Professional or Individual. You may want to view the available and eligible categories, before clicking on the button to check the variety of product categories that you may list with each account type.

Step 3

Fill out relevant information. On this page, keep your eye on the Amazon Services Agreement. Take your time in reading it before checking the box that you have accepted the terms and conditions. Creating an account as an Individual seller has somewhat a straightforward process with less information needed unlike registering the Professional account. Just a bit of suggestion when making your Store Name, think of a name about "quality deals" so that your Amazon Storefront would reflect a shopper friendly store.

Add to your name words like: Best ever, Deals, Discount, Quality, For less, Specialty, Fast, Great and similar that you can think of.

Step 4

When you click the "Continue" button, you'll provide the information needed for phone verification. Choose whether you want to be called or sent a text message to the phone number you entered. You'll be given a 4-digit pin which you will type in to verify your identity.

Step 5

Click the "Register" button and your registration will be complete. If you already have a shopping Amazon account, you may directly login to that account to register the Amazon seller account by clicking the Your Seller Account. In fact, you may use the same information from your buyer account to register as Individual seller.

It's that easy, right? Amazon makes everything easy. What's more? Well, you can now join the Amazon FBA program: the reason why this book is written.

FBA program is one of the great benefits of being an Amazon seller to gain customers and boost sales. Any seller can try the FBA program and initially test it with few products to send to Amazon.

It is advisable to make use of this program as soon as you become an Amazon seller. Adding Fulfillment by Amazon to selling on Amazon account is a quick process. Here's an illustration you can easily follow to set an item to be fulfilled by Amazon. With Amazon FBA, every step is towards growing your business!

Though fees in FBA may be higher, the products will sell much faster so it will make greater profits. FBA fees are only offset by the costs you may incur when you ship it yourself. I know as a businessperson, you want to save more time. Aside from saving your time from packing, you can expect to have a reliable venue in managing your inventory. There are tasks that can automatically do it for you. Just set up your Seller Central account and sign up for value-added services.

Recommended Amazon Seller Settings

As early as now, it is better that you'll have an idea of what needs to be done to set up onto the FBA account settings as soon as you sign up your seller account.

I hope this will make you feel relaxed because what I will share with you now can actually save your energy and time, rather than do drudging administrative tasks of selling online.

Moreover, it will increase efficiency when Amazon is fulfilling customer orders. The most recommended account settings to be enabled are the Automated Unfulfillable Removal Settings and Restricted Items Warning. These settings are important in saving your time so you can focus on other matters of your business. Here's what you need to know about these settings:

1. **Automated Unfulfillable Removal Setting**
   Automatically manages your unfulfillable units, whether you choose to return or dispose of as you scheduled. It saves time in managing products that are damaged or not being fulfilled.

2. **Show Restricted Items Warning**
   Keeps you alerted about FBA product restrictions. You don't need to check from time to time if the product which needs shipping to Amazon is restricted or not. It helps to manage your listing according to the suitable products to list with Amazon FBA. Not only that! There are other two account settings that may be optional, but surely are favorable to you if you enable it on your account.

3. Stickerless, Commingled Inventory Settings

Enable you not to label the products you send to Amazon but instead, use the existing barcodes. What Amazon does is combining the identical inventory of Amazon or other sellers in the fulfillment centers. Therefore, whenever there are orders to fulfill, Amazon does not need to physically distinguish your inventory from others. Consequently, it makes order processing more efficient and will benefit you as a seller.

4. Inventory Placement

Allows you to split your shipments to different fulfillment centers because certain types of products have specialized fulfillment centers. If your products are properly distributed, there is assurance that delivery lead time can be fulfilled effectively. Done with signing up! By this time, the determination to pursue your Amazon selling business should be alive!

Chapter 5:

How to market with Ads?

In this chapter, we will talk about Facebook ads and Instagram ads. Allowing you to understand how to use them in terms of making them useful for your Amazon FBA business.

Facebook Ads

The method of how to market your ads will remain the same for both Instagram and Facebook.

Using Facebook Ads Manager

Do you want to start a Facebook ad but aren't sure where to begin? That's a common feeling, which is why this entire chapter is dedicated to the process of creating an ad. However, before you can run an ad campaign on Facebook, you must learn about the Facebook Ads Manager. It's a great tool that you can't do without when growing your business.

Create an account on the Ads Manager

The first step is to learn how to set up an account on the Ads Manager. To get started, you must log into your Facebook account, open the drop-down menu present on the upper right corner of your account, and click on the "Create Ads" option. This will open an account for you and will help you set up and run your ad campaign on Facebook.

Explore Ads Manager

Once you open the main menu in the Ads Manager, you can see different options: Plan, Measure & Report, Assets, Create & Manage, and Settings.

Once you start using Ads Manager frequently, you will notice another section, the "Frequently Used" section, where you can easily find all the tools you regularly use. Below are all the tools you will become familiar with when using the Ads Manager.

Plan

The "Plan" section includes tools to help you understand your target audience and give you ideas for running Facebook ads.

The "Audience Insights" tool in this section will help you find all the information you need about your target audience on Facebook. It also allows you to create a custom audience based on things such as user interests, gender, age group, location as well as the pages they like.

According to the parameters you select, Facebook Ads Manager will give you the necessary information you will need. For instance, you can discover helpful advertising ideas when you ask Facebook to provide data about those users who like your Facebook page.

You must first input information in Audience Insights for the information you need about the users who like your page. Based on the parameters you select, Insights will display various tabs about those users.

The first tab of information is related to demographics. The graph produced in this section will provide information about the age and gender of all the users who like your page. The demographic data also provides information about users' professions, marital status, and qualifications. Using this information, you can create content that will appeal to them.

When you open the "Page Likes" option in the Insights report, you can see data that will come in handy while creating content for your target audience. For instance, within an ad campaign, you can create different ads that target the segments of your audience based on the pages that they like or follow.

If you are aware of the kind of pages they like and what those pages offer, you can create ads that will appeal to your audience.

Check all the information displayed under various tabs apart from "Demographics" and "Page Likes" to learn more about your target audience. For instance, you can discover data related to the users' location, level of engagement on Facebook, household income, and purchases.

You can also use this to analyze your custom audience and their specific interests. For instance, if the users who like your page also like another page on Facebook and you wish to learn more about the particular page, then you can ask Audience Insights to provide you the data of that page by including it in your interest option.

Another tool in the Plan section is the "Creative Hub". You can use this to create mockups of your ad and share it with others to get their feedback or any other ideas.

Frequently Used

As the name suggests, this section shows the four most frequently used tools. Think of it as a quick action LaunchPad.

If you don't see a specific tool you want to use, like the "Audience Insights", then you must click on the "All Tools" option, and you will be able to see a list of all the tools available.

Create and Manage

In this section, you will find the tools you need for creating and managing ad campaigns on Facebook.

The Business Manager tool will come in handy if you have an advertising team or are using more than one page. If you sign up for "Business Manager" then it lends structure as well as organization to your Ads Manager account. You cannot access this tool without signing up for it.

The Ads Manager tool will help run the ad campaigns and also analyze the data from those campaigns.

You can use Facebook Pixel and download the customized reports from it for further analysis.

The Power Editor is a brilliant advertising tool that helps you create ad campaigns. When creating ads, this tool offers different advanced features and options like running an ad on a schedule set according to the time zones, controlling the placement of the ad, optimizing the ad to increase engagement rate or impressions, bulk uploading, and running unpublished posts.

The Page Posts tool helps you view all the posts on your page and the way the users are interacting with the content you post. Different options like Scheduled Posts, Ads Posts, and Published Posts are available in this tool. You can also view data about the reach of your post, the total clicks or engagement generated per post, the number of users who took action, and the date of publishing.

If you want to direct the traffic to your app (provided you have one) to increase the downloads, you can use the App Ads Helper.

Another interesting feature in the "Create & Manage" section is the Automated Rules. Use this option to establish certain rules for your ad campaigns. It also helps you automate alerts or perform a specific action when the rules you set are met. For instance, you can set the rule to automatically stop an ad if its CPC, or cost per conversion, exceeds $5. If according to the tool's estimates, the CPC of your ad increases beyond $5, then the ad will stop being published until you review it. By doing this, you can forego the need to constantly check your daily ad budgets. While creating rules, you have different parameters to adjust like the application of the rule you set, the way you want to receive notifications, the automatic action to be taken when the rule is met, and the frequency of the application of the rule, and the different conditions to be met.

Measure and Report

If you want to analyze how your ad campaign is doing, then you need to access the Measure & Report section of the Ads Manager.

You can access various tools in this section like Ads Reporting, Custom Conversions, and Analytics.

The Ads Reporting tool helps generate a report for an ad you are running. If you want to analyze any previous ads, you can set the date or the time frame within which the ads will run. By analyzing the ads you run, you can create better ads in the future. If you want to compare various campaigns and analyze the different metrics of key performance, then this tool comes in handy. For instance, if the key performance metric you want to analyze the ads on is the click-through rate or the cost per conversion, you can use this tool.

Facebook Pixel automatically tracks certain key metrics related to the actions different users take on your website like viewing the content. Having a custom Facebook Pixel conversion will help you track specific actions (you can define this action) the users take.

The Custom Conversions tool, as the name suggests, helps create custom conversions, and you can also view all the custom conversions you created in the past. Custom Conversions enables marketers to track as well as to optimize conversions without having to add anything extra to the Facebook Pixel code on the site. You can also check when you received the pixel data and the custom conversions that are active now.

You can include 40 custom conversions per ad account. To create a new custom conversion for tracking the activity on your website, you must click on the "Create Custom Conversion" option and fill in the necessary information in the popup menu. While doing this, you need to include a URL in the rule for tracking the activity. Once you create the custom conversion, you can generate a custom conversion ad and then select the custom conversions you wish to track for determining the success of the ad. For instance, if the users who register themselves on your website are directed to a Thank You page, then place the Thank You page's URL in the Rule tab. This will ensure that whenever a user registers themselves and is directed to the Thank You page, the pixel records the action and notifies Facebook about the genuine conversion. After you create a custom conversion, refresh the page to enable the custom conversion.

The Analytics tool will enable you to analyze the data generated from your page and Facebook Pixel. As you create ads and work with the pixel, Analytics is a rather helpful tool that will optimize your marketing efforts on Facebook.

Assets

Another option in the main menu of the Ads Manager is Assets. This option gives you quick and easy access to all the important assets you used for creating your ads, including the images you used, data from the Facebook Pixel and your target audience, and much more. The different tools available in this section are Audience, Pixels, and Offline Events.

The Audience tool allows you to create a custom audience while designing the ad. This tool also comes in handy while establishing your target audience for any future ads. If you want, you can save an audience, and you can access this while creating other ads too. You can create three types of audiences according to Facebook, and they are a custom audience, lookalike and saved audience.

Custom audience refers to the kind of audience you are targeting according to certain parameters of your choice. A lookalike audience refers to an audience who shares similarities with your custom audience. Once you use a specific audience for creating an ad, you can save that specific audience for future reference.

According to your ad campaign objective, you can select a specific type of audience. For instance, according to the user's engagement on your website, Facebook page, or app, you can create a custom audience.

Once you've select the kind of custom audience, Facebook will guide you through all the options available. For instance, if you want to create your custom audience according to their Facebook engagement, you can select the different types of engagement you want to consider. You can target audiences according to different parameters like those who viewed your videos, the ones who engaged with your page, or those who clicked on an ad.

Once you set an engagement option, you need to select the specific interactions you wish to target. This means you can narrow down the options for your custom audience by setting specific ways in which you can define the audience you wish to target like interactions related to your page.

The custom audience option allows you to target all those users with whom you have had some interaction in the past whereas the lookalike audience option allows you to find other users who share attributes similar to the ones of your existing audience.

Once you select the lookalike audience option, click on the Source option to guide Facebook about the specific attributes you are looking for in users.

After you do this, you must define two parameters, and which are the location of the audience and the audience size.

The Images option allows you to see the images you used in a recent ad or anything you might have picked up from other posts. The list of images displayed is sorted according to their recent use.

The pixel option allows you to insert a Facebook Pixel or see the data obtained from any pixels you used in the past. You can use the pixel data to create better ads. For instance, if you notice that a specific post obtained a lot of views, then you can create an ad targeting those users who read the post and provide them a content upgrade if they provide their email address. It is a simple means of increasing your email list.

An Offline Event is a tool which helps you track all the activity that takes place outside Facebook. For instance, if someone who saw your ad on Facebook visits your physical store to make a purchase, this information will be included in this tool. If you want to create an offline event, you must input the customer data and compare it against all those who viewed your online ad.

The Settings tool is where all your basic account information is stored like payment information, email address, and any other particulars related to your account.

Instagram Ads

Instagram gets over one billion visitors each month. In addition to this, the numbers of engagement for this application is way more than Twitter and Facebook combined. This means you are losing out big time if you are not taking advantage of what the app has to offer. This is the reason why this chapter will be teaching you how Instagram advertising works, and all the vital information regarding Instagram ads, so you can get your content across to the individuals on Instagram who matter to you. But first, we will be looking into what Instagram ad is.

Limited ad services were first introduced by Instagram when Facebook took over it in 2013. However, it only began to provide advertising access to various sizes of businesses and brands in 2015.

These brands soon realized that Instagram was of enormous benefit for businesses. Also, because Instagram is incorporated with Facebook Ads Manager, brands can take advantage of the enormous resources of user data Facebook offers to advertise right to the audience they desire.

If you prefer numbers to understand how beneficial Instagram ads can be, below are a few statistics:

- 75% of the Instagram users perform an action via Instagram ads like heading to a site or buying a product;
- 35% of adults in America utilize Instagram.

In essence, if you are not taking advantage of Instagram ads, you are depriving yourself of a considerable amount of possible revenue.

What is the cost of Instagram ads?

Depending on your ad objectives, the cost may be unique to you. This is because all ads differ.

However, for Instagram ads, the typical CPC (cost-per-click) is about $0.70 – $0.80.

This figure was obtained from an evaluation of over $300million spent on ads.

Note that this is just like an estimate. You may end up spending more or less depending on numerous factors such as the time of the year ads are set-up.

Creating ads on Instagram

Now that you understand the basics, we will be taking a look at how to create ads. We will be learning to do it using the Facebook Ad Manager, which is a prevalent method because it is easy to use.

It also offers you the capacity to personalize your ad more than you would if you were using the application itself. Below are the steps that can help you create your ad. Head to the Ad Manager via Facebook.

Presuming you already have a Facebook account, and you are logged in, all you need to do is follow this link to get to the Facebook Ad Manager. There is no precise Instagram Ad Manager. You oversee Instagram ads via the Facebook Ads UI.

Determine your marketing goals

Here, you need to pick a campaign goal. The great news is that the goals are clearly stated. If you are after additional traffic, select the traffic goal. If you want more engagement, choose the engagement goal, and so on. However, there are only a few goals you can work with using Instagram ads, which include:

- Traffic
- Brand awareness
- Video Views
- Engagement
- Conversions
- Reach
- App Installs

Determine your target audience

After determining your objective, you have to target the right audience so your ad gets to the appropriate individuals. This is where Instagram ads flourish since you will be utilizing the demographic knowledge, Facebook offers to get to the right individuals.

If you have previously utilized Facebook ads, you may have already built some audiences and understand the entire process. If you are using it for the first time, below are the targeting options you have at your disposal, you can narrow them down to reach a specific audience.

For example, if you want to target men in Chicago, between the age of 18- 25, who have an interest in sporting equipment, you will have the capacity to do that. The targeting actions include:

- Location: lets you target a city, state, country, or zip code and ignore specific areas;
- Gender: pick between all genders, or only men and vice versa;
- Age: lets you target different age ranges;
- Demographics: you can access this under "Detailed Targeting". It also has numerous sub-categories to pick from.
- Languages: Facebook suggests that you leave this place blank unless the language you want to target is not typical in the area you are aiming to target.
- Behaviors: this is also an option you will find under "Detailed Targeting". It also provides you with numerous categories to check out. It could either be anniversaries, purchasing behaviors, job roles, and a host of other options.
- Interests: another option you will have access to under "Detailed Targeting" which offers numerous sub-categories to delve into. If you are in search of

individuals who have an interest in horror movies, or beverages, you get these options and many more.

- Custom Audience: with this option, you will be able to upload your contact list and target leads or clients who you aim to upsell.
- Lookalike Audience: here, Instagram gives you the chance to locate audiences who share lots of similarities to your other audiences.
- Connections: here, you can target individuals connected to your app, page, or event.

After configuring your audience, Facebook also offers you a guide on how broad or specific your audience is. It is vital you take note of this because you want to choose a point where your audience is not too broad since it is not adequately targeted, but you don't want it to be too narrow either, since you may be unable to reach that many individuals.

Determine your placements

The next step after targeting the demographic of your choice is to select your placement. This is vital if your campaign objectives are to show the ads on Instagram alone. If you decide to skip this step, Facebook will let your ads show up on the two platforms. This can be a positive thing, but if you have created content for Instagram specifically, you need to pick the option "Edit Placements."

From this point, you can choose Instagram as your placement, and if you would prefer the ads to show up on the stories or feed area of the platform. You also have the option of letting it show up on both.

Determine your Ad schedule and budget

If you understand how budgets work via AdWords, Facebook, and other platforms for running an ad, you may not have any issues with this step. If you have not, then it is not so much of a problem either, even though you may not understand how to put your lifetime or daily budget in place while running an Instagram campaign for the first time, you learn on the go. What's more, you also can pause or stop your ad at any point, if you believe your budget is not being apportioned the right way.

So which should you go with? A daily or lifetime budget? This is solely dependent on you, but if you decide to go with a daily budget, it ensures your budget does not get exhausted fast. In contrast, a lifetime budget gives you

84

the capacity for scheduling your ad delivery. Both options do the work they should, so it is a matter of choice. As mentioned earlier, you can schedule an ad to target certain moments of the week or day, that experience peak activity from your audience. If you are utilizing a lifetime budget, this can be an essential way of optimizing your budget.

Develop your Instagram Ad

Here comes the moment you need to create your ad. Here, the set-up may seem different based on the objective you decide to go with. There are six ad formats that Instagram provides you with.

From the options provided, two show up on Instagram stories, while the other four show up on your Instagram feed. The latter is the option many marketers and advertisers take advantage of. The options available include:

- Image Feed ads
- Image Story ads
- Video Feed ads
- Video Story ads
- Carousel Feed ads

- Canvas Story ads

Each one of these ad formats is incorporated into the Stories and Feeds of the users which offer a non-distracting experience for users. Instagram also provides you with a range of call-to-actions that can aid you in attaining more leads. We will be taking a look at each of them below:

Image Feed Ads

This is the most common ad format, and, if you frequently use Instagram, there is a huge possibility that you may have come across it while perusing your feed. These ads consist of a single image that shows up when your target audience is going through their feed. The great thing about this ad is that if you do them properly, they will look like any other feed instead of ads. Some of the specifications for this ad include:

- Type of file: Jpeg or PNG
- Max size of the file: 30MB
- Number of Hashtags: Maximum of 30
- Length of Text: 2,200 max.

However, for the best delivery, Instagram suggests you stay below 90 characters.

Image Story Ads

This is similar to the Image Feed ads, but they show up on the Instagram Stories of your target. The specifications include 9:16 recommended image ratio and no less than 600 pixels' image width.

Video Feed Ads

You can give your ad more life using a video. If you create a video of high quality, then it is possible to promote it via your Instagram feed. Instagram offers support for various video files, but it is suggested that you use:

- Square pixels;
- Progressive scan;
- Fixed frame rate;
- H.264 compression;
- 128kbps+ stereo AAC audio compression.

However, if you do have a video that fails to meet these requirements, numerous apps can aid you in altering your video. Some of the specifications for video feed ads include:

- Video resolution: No less than 1080 x 1080 pixels'
- Max file size: 4GB
- Max length of video: 60 seconds
- 125 characters' text length recommended
- Number of Hashtags: Maximum 30

Video Story Ads

Stories are also great locations for running ads. This is because lots of users often expect to see videos here so it may not come as a surprise to see ads. The specifications for these ads are listed below:

- Video Resolution: No less than 1080 x 1920 pixels
- Video Length: Maximum 15 seconds
- Maximum file size: 4GB

Carousel Feed Ads

Depending on how you use it, this format of ads can be quite fun. It lets you display a group of images users can scroll through instead of just one image.

This kind of ad is ideal for brands that are very visual like those in the clothing industry, travel industry, food industry, and vehicle industry, among others.

You can use this to show your audience the faces behind your organization. The carousel feed ads let you include as much as ten images in one ad, all with a link to each product. Also, you have the option of adding a video to this form of ad. The specifications for this ad are:

- Type of file: JPG or PNG
- Number of Hashtags: Maximum 30
- Length of Text: 2,200 max. However, for the best delivery, Instagram suggests you stay below 90 characters.
- Max file size: 30MB
- Length of Video: Maximum 60 seconds

Canvas Story Ads

Finally, the most recent inclusion of the ad formats is Canvas ads. With these ads, you can create a VR experience in your story. They only function on mobile devices and give you complete control of customization options. However, you need some technical knowledge.

These ads can work alongside video, image, and carousel. The specifications for this format are:

- Minimum width of the image: 400 pixels
- Max Height of Image: 150 pixels

Determining the best Ad format to use

You need to determine the best format for your needs and the question below can help you make a choice: what is your objective?

Your desired social media objective is the foundation for all the conclusions you make when it has to do with an ad campaign. It will aid you in determining what you should focus on and what you should not. Any ad you choose has to align with your objectives, always remember that.

Chapter 6:
AMS ads

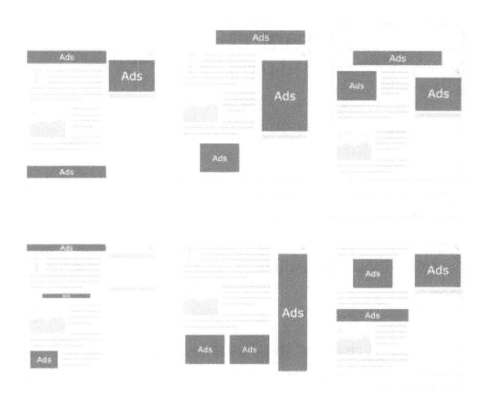

In which you make decisions that seem trivial or inconsequential at the time, but that can have an enduring impact on your ad tracking, sales, and management.

If you're new to AMS ads, read this chapter before moving on! If you've been running ads for a while, you can skip this chapter if you choose, as you've probably already learned all this the hard way.

The AMS dashboard

To access the AMS dashboard, go to:

https://advertising.amazon.com/ads/dashboard

Alternatively, you can reach the dashboard from your FBA dashboard, go to:

Reports > Ad Campaigns > view your ads dashboard page

After you've reached the dashboard, you'll see a bright yellow button at the top left that says "New Campaign." That's what you'll select to create a campaign. But don't get click just yet!
You have a few decisions to make before you dive in.

Sponsored Product ads vs Product Display ads

We'll be discussing Sponsored Product (keyword) ads, not Product Display ads. Why?

Because you can make use of them with minimal investment. Remember, this is AMS ads for the rest of us.

We're looking for methods that will work for the majority. Product Display ads have provided a good return for a few sellers of my acquaintance, and they may work for you, but they require a large budget and they can spend money in a heartbeat.

I learned that lesson: one day I didn't check one of my Product Display ads for 24 hours and it burned through $96 with no sales to show for it.

Sponsored Product ads, on the other hand, can run with a daily budget of $1, so they won't suddenly bleed you dry. This minimal investment gives you room to play when it comes to testing, tweaking, and pivoting on the fly. You can pause your ads, or increase/decrease the daily spend at any time, allowing you to manage costs if your marketing budget expands or contracts.

Naming your ad campaigns

This might seem like a minor point, but believe me, it becomes critical the more campaigns you run, especially if you plan to keep older drives going.

Now, you're confronted with a text box that offers the example of "Holiday Favorites."

DON'T let that trick you into using something that generic. If you do, your ads are likely to become as chaotic as a room full of Tribbles.

You'll want to create a naming convention for your ads that will help you keep things organized without adding extra work. Trust me on this. Pick a naming convention and stick with it.

How should you name your ads? That depends on what information will help you quickly and easily identify specific ads. I came up with an alphanumeric combination for mine that reflects the series and where each product slots into the sequence.

For example, I designated SR for my Starhawke Rising series and SRO for my upcoming Starhawk Rogue series. This will allow me to use the campaign name to quickly sort my ads by series, with all the SR ads grouped, followed by the SRO ads.

I also include the number of the product in the series, for example, SR3 if I'm running an ad for the third product in the Starhawk Rising series. Finally, I include whatever terms let me know what types of keywords the ad is using, for instance, "Space Opera sellers."

The complete campaign name would end up being something like "SR3 Space Opera sellers."

You can include whatever information is relevant to you, but I recommend keeping it short, about 20-23 characters max, so the full name will show in the AMS ads dashboard.

One of my seller friends uses the first line of her ad copy as her naming system, which gives her an easy way to compare the results for different ads that are using the same ad copy.

As you proceed through this chapter, start mulling over what conventions will help you know at a glance which product you're advertising and how you've targeted the ad.

Start and End dates

Unless you're running your ad to coincide with a timed promotion, I recommend using the "No end date" option when creating a new campaign. If the ad's doing poorly, you can always terminate it. If it's doing well, you'll want to keep it going rather than having it end on a pre-specified date.

For my first two ads, I accidentally set an expiration date for about three months in the future. As these have been two very effective ads, I've kept them running well past their expiration date. But because I set that date range, I have to remember to go into the dashboard every few months and extend the expiration date to prevent them from being terminated. It's a hassle. Unless you have a compelling reason to set a date range, go with the default "No end date" option to have your ads run continuously.

If you're wondering why I haven't just created new ads to replace the originals using the same keywords, bids, etc., so I can terminate the older ones, the answer is simple: it won't work!

No twosome ads will ever run at the same, even if they're identical. And if you think like an algorithm, it's not hard to understand why. Imagine you go to the grocery store every Friday at 9 am. You always take the same route, starting and ending at the same place, but no matter how hard you try, you will never have precisely the same experience. Each time you will encounter different people, potential obstacles, or unexpected boosts. One day it might be raining, another there might be an accident you have to avoid, while on another you may be the only one on the road and cut your travel time in half. The same is true about AMS ads.

When you start an ad, you have no way to predict what it will encounter on its journey because the conditions are always changing. It might hit a traffic jam of other ads and never get shown. Or, it might get shown but not get clicks or generate sales because your ideal readers aren't buying that day. And if you don't get a similar initial response to the duplicate ad, it may languish in obscurity.

I know this from experience because I tried exactly that, creating duplicate ads to replace the ones with the expiration date. They did okay, well enough to last for a few months before I terminated them. But they failed to repeat the success of the originals.

Ad Copy: image and custom text

One distinctive advantage of AMS ads versus other advertising platforms is you don't have to come up with an image. Your product cover is your image, so as long as you've done your due diligence crafting a suitable shelter, that part's a no-brainer. And, if you choose to, you can even run an ad without custom ad copy or keywords.

Very simple. However, I don't recommend it. Without ad copy or keywords, you're losing out on the opportunity to hook potential readers. You're the writer, after all. You understand the power of words. The text that appears in your ad needs to entice the reader to click, moving them from the ad to your product's sales page. You have 150 characters to work with (including spaces), so every one of them needs to count.

Per Amazon's Ad Specs and Policies, your ad must NOT contain any of the following:

- Ending of sentences with punctuation marks other than a period;
- Single question mark;
- Exclamation mark (no using !!! to make it more enticing to the potential reader);
- Special characters or symbols, including legal symbols Email addresses or website URLs Ending with article words (the, a, an);
- ALL CAPS except for well-known abbreviations (YA for young adult is acceptable, BUY NOW is not);
- Pricing messages (no "99 cents!");

- Reference to the Amazon rating score (no "4.6 stars!");
- Overly forceful phrases or exclamation points (don't use "Don't miss out!", "HURRY - SAVE NOW");
- Special offers, promotions or contests;
- Customer reviews unless the specific review is contained in the product description on the detail page;
- Third-party customer reviews or rating scores
- Emotionally draining or depressing messages
- Foul, vulgar or obscene language

If you violate any of these guidelines, your ad will be rejected, and you'll have to start over.

As a bonus, that rejected ad will sit cluttering up your AMS dashboard until the end of time. Save yourself the effort and frustration by going over this list before submitting your ad.

What should you use for ad copy? There are entire courses taught on this topic, so I'll only touch on it here. For AMS ads, you're dealing with just 150 characters. A variation of the tagline from your product description may be all you need.

Not sure whether you have a good tagline, or which tagline from several options is most effective? AMS ads can help you test that out. You can create a set of ads with the same keywords but different ad copy and see which ads do well and which ones flop. Experimentation is the key. You never know what will strike a chord with potential readers until you test, test, test.

How, exactly, do you create that test? First, finish this product! You'll want to have all the information I've provided at your disposal before you try this experiment. When you're ready, follow the steps below.

Create two (or more) ads with identical bids, daily budgets, and keywords, but with different copy for each ad. Start them at the same time and then monitor the results for 1-3 weeks, depending on your budget and your patience. Which one gets the most impressions? The most clicks? The most sales? When you think you've found your winner, pause the other ad(s) in the set and see if the remaining ad continues to perform well. If it does, congratulations! You've found your winning ad copy.

If the leading ad falters after you pause the others, enable all the ads in the set, and monitor for another 1-2 weeks to pick out your winner.

You can pause or terminate any ad that is a dud before the test is over. You may also find that you have two or more ads that do well, acting as a tag-team, with one performing stronger for a while and then the other. In that case, by all means, keep them both running!

Keywords

Perhaps the most deceptively simple and yet incredibly complex concept in marketing. Keywords will make or break your ads.

If you can learn to view them as trusted friends rather than skulking adversaries, you'll see how they can be incredibly gifted teachers and the perfect sales team for your product.

What is a keyword? For the purposes of AMS ads, keywords refer to seller names, product titles, series titles, and other genre-related words or phrases that help Amazon's algorithm put your product in front of the right audience.

Audrey Sharpe, The Dark of Light, Starhawke Rising, and space opera are all examples of keywords.

Automatic or Manual targeting?

When you create your AMS ads, you'll have two choices: Automatic targeting or Manual targeting. When adding your list of keywords, you'll want to choose the manual keyword targeting option. That's not to say you should never create an ad using Amazon's Automatic targeting. You may find the algorithm does a fabulous job of targeting your ideal reader, especially if your cover, tagline, and product description are optimized to attract the right audience. But in this product, we're focusing on creating manual keyword ads.

Where do you find keywords?

In my experience, the best keywords for AMS ads are seller's names. Product titles, series titles, and other keywords can produce results but expect about 80-90% of your top keywords to be seller names. It pays to start there when gathering your keyword lists. You'll notice I said lists, plural. Don't expect to have just one list.

Various lists from multiple sources give you flexibility. You have no way to know until you test which sets of keywords will produce results, so the more variety you can gather, the better.

There's some debate as to whether each ad's keywords need to be a cohesive set (for example, all space opera sellers) or whether a hodge-podge will do the trick just as well or better. While I organize my keyword lists by type (space opera sellers, cowboy sellers, space opera bestsellers, etc.), and will run some ads with keywords taken from just one list, many of my more successful ads are a hodge-podge of the best keywords from multiple directories.

Testing will help you determine what works for you.

Where do you go to compile your lists?

I'm so glad you asked!

1. "Also Bought"

   Look for these on your product page. They're the products that show under the heading "Customers who bought this item also bought," hence the term also bought, or the also shortened bots.

   For years, the "also bought" were listed underneath the product description, but Amazon has been testing new layouts and placement, so you may have to hunt a bit to find them.

"Also bought" are an excellent source for keywords because you know for a fact a reader purchased both your product and the one listed in your "also bought" list. That means statistically there's a good chance other readers who like that seller will enjoy your product too. However, beware of making assumptions!

Outliers that don't belong in your genre do pop up in "also bought" and can lead you astray. If you follow them blindly, you may suffer the consequences. Focus on seller names, product titles, and series names for a product in your "also bought" that fit in the same categories as the product you're promoting.

2. Yasiv.com

This resource is excellent for those who like visuals. After you enter the title of your product or your seller name, you'll see a map showing you all the products that are connected to yours either directly or tangentially. The list might be small when the product's a new release, but it will grow over time. Hopefully, it will be populated with the product you believe your ideal reader will enjoy. If it's not, you know you have some work to do to target your perfect reader, possibly including tweaking your cover, tag line, and product description.

As with the "also bought", you'll want to make a list of the seller names, titles, and series titles for the product that are a good match for yours. Avoid any product you don't think your ideal reader would enjoy. They're especially helpful if you're doing your first AMS ads in a new-to-you genre where you're not sure which sellers to target. Not only are you likely to generate sales from these lists, but you'll gain valuable marketing insight into your genre at the same time.

To access these lists, select the genre links in the Amazon sidebar to reach your chosen subgenre (for example General & Electronics > iPhones> iPhone XS).

When you're on that page, under the "refine by" options in the sidebar, locate the seller's section. It shows a shortlist of about ten sellers followed by a blue link that says "See more."

Click on the "See more" link. You will be taken to page one of a listing for all sellers Amazon has associated with that genre.

A little copying, pasting and editing to remove the number after each name (which denotes how many titles the seller has in that subgenre) will produce outstanding lists of seller keywords targeted to your subgenre. You'll find time-saving instructions for the copying and pasting process in the Afterword.

3. Subgenre bestseller lists

As with the "Also Bought", this will be a list of seller names, product titles and series titles. However, this is a broader net than your "Also Bought" and Yasiv, because there's no direct connection to your product other than a genre.

Also, the sellers you're seeing are bestsellers, so you'll probably have to spend more on these keywords for them to be effective.

4. Promotional newsletters

This is a slow build list that can be compiled over time by signing up for promotional newsletters like the product but, targeting the genres you write in. On a daily/weekly/monthly basis, go through those newsletters and pull out seller names, product titles, and series titles for a product that you think your ideal reader would enjoy. For extra credit, take a screenshot of the entire ad copy for that product and save it in a folder. Analyzing what the seller did right to attract your attention can be a gold mine for inspiration when it comes time to write your product description and ad copy or to design your cover.

Does spelling count? Yes! But not necessarily the way you think. When creating your ads, brainstorm all the possible alternate spellings for sellers you know are good targets for your subgenre, especially if they have a name with several common spellings.

You'll never know which one will produce the most views and clicks for your ads until you test them out. Often, you'll find that misspelling a seller's name will make it a more effective keyword.

My mom's a great example. She spells her first name Vicki with an "I," but there are a lot of readers who type it into Amazon's search bar as Vicky or Vickie. In fact, after targeting these alternate spellings of her seller name in her AMS ads, I've discovered that the misspellings produce better results than the correct spelling. I should also point out that some sellers choose not to target their seller name, product titles, and series titles in their AMS ads. The reasoning is that your product should show automatically when a reader types in your name or product title in the search bar.

If the reader clicks on the search result, it doesn't cost you anything, but if you use your name/title/series as a keyword in your ads and they click on the sponsored ad instead (which usually shows above the search result listing for the product), it costs you money unnecessarily.

I understand the logic, however, in my experience with my mom's ads, the keywords for her seller name consistently perform well across the board, earning significantly more than the cost for their clicks.

Yes, she may have gotten those sales anyway without the ads, but I think part of the reason it's useful for her is that she has an extensive catalog.

If her ads show in the sponsored ads slots on the search results page for her seller/title/series rather than another seller's ads, then that significantly decreases the chances that a reader will click away to someone else's product rather than buying one of hers.

If you don't use your seller name as a keyword in your ads, you're ceding those slots on your search results page to other sellers. Which choice is right for you? The only way to find out is to test and compare the results.

If you're targeting a seller who uses initials instead of a name, try entering the initials in different combinations that include or exclude the punctuation or spaces. You might be surprised by how differently they'll perform. The most effective keyword I've ever had from any of my lists, the one that has earned more than twice as much as the next closest keyword, is a seller name where the seller uses initials. However, the correct spelling of her name with periods after the initials weren't producing any results. Zero.

I knew she was a good fit for the subgenre I was targeting, so I tried a variation where I removed the two periods, and voila!

She rocketed to the top of the list and has stayed there for almost a year. Punctuation can get in the way with titles, too.

For example, "Honors Flight" without the apostrophe might perform better than "Honor's Flight", even though the punctuation isn't grammatically correct, and it doesn't exactly match the product title.

However, the system doesn't care about capitalization. You couldn't enter "Audrey Sharpe" and "audrey sharpe" as keywords for the same ad, because the system sees them as identical. With all your keywords, keep in mind that you're attempting to match what a reader is typing in the search bar. There's no guarantee they know the correct spellings or even the right name and title for your product. Your goal is to figure out what they're typing in so you can use those spellings and phrases as effective keywords for your ads. Suggested, Enter Keywords, and Upload File For each advertisement, you'll have the option to enter keywords in three different ways.

<u>Suggested</u>

These are keywords Amazon has come up with that you have the option to add to your campaign. They're usually variations of your title, series name, genre, and number in series. I've never had much success with these keywords in the ads I've run, but others have found some gems in the mix. By all means, add the ones you like and see how they do!

Enter Keywords

This is the best option for those who would like to manually add individual keywords or copy and paste a list of keywords from a Word or other text document. To add from a text document, make sure each keyword in the list is on a new line, then click and drag your cursor to highlight them all (make them blue) and select copy (CTRL+C on your keyboard). Next, click on the AMS ads text box that says Enter keywords separated by a new line, and paste in the keywords (CTRL+V on your keyboard). Your keywords will appear in a list in the text box. Click on the "Add keywords" button to add the keywords to your campaign.

Upload File

For those comfortable with Excel, you can download the Keyword Bulk Upload XLSX template file. Add your keywords, match type, and bids to the template and upload in bulk.

Broad, Phrase, or Exact?

This is a new feature Amazon launched in August 2018. I haven't had a chance to gather test results yet, but I'll give you the basic rundown of what the three terms mean concerning your keywords.

Broad

This setting is how keyword ads have been working since the beginning. Whatever keywords you enter, Amazon's algorithm will try matching them in any order, including plurals, variables, and related keywords.

Phrase

This setting means you only want Amazon to match the keyword if what the potential reader types into the search box contains the exact phrase or sequence of words you entered. For example, if I set Audrey Sharpe as a keyword with the Phrase setting, then if someone typed in Audrey Sharpe Starhawke series into the search bar, the keyword would be a match. However, if they typed in Sharpe Starhawke seller, it would not. This setting limits the potential matches for your keyword.

Exact

In this instance, what the possible reader types must match the keyword or phrase exactly. No more, no less.

This setting severely limits the possible matches for your keyword.

Why would you want to limit your keyword settings? One example would be if you're targeting a seller who has a name similar to another seller in a different genre, and you want to limit how often your ad might be shown to the wrong audience. My mom's a case in point. She writes contemporary romance as Vicki Lewis Thompson, but there's also a Victoria Thompson on Amazon who writes historical mysteries.

To their fans, they're both known as Vicki Thompson. If you used the Broad setting for the keyword Vicki Lewis Thompson or Victoria Thompson in your ad, it's possible Amazon's algorithm would show your ad to any reader who types in Vicki Thompson. But if you changed the setting to Phrase or Exact, then the reader would have to type in Vicki Lewis Thompson or Victoria Thompson to get a match and be shown the ad. That's the advantage. On the downside, if you were targeting my mom and used Phrase or Exact, you'd lose out on anyone who was searching for her product and left out the Lewis when typing her name in the search box.

Negative keywords

This is another new feature Amazon rolled out in August 2018. The goal of using negative keywords is to prevent your ad from being shown to people who aren't likely to buy your product. This can help reduce your advertising costs by excluding your ad from irrelevant searches. For example, since I have a metaphysical space opera adventure series,

I might use the space opera as an ad keyword. However, I could enter military sci-fi as a negative keyword for my ads so they won't be shown to anyone typing military sci-fi space opera into Amazon's search box. While some folks who are interested in android might like iPhones, they're not my target audience. I don't want to spend a bunch of money showing them my ads. The same might be true if you have sellers in your chosen subgenre that you know aren't likely to appeal to your ideal readers. Adding their names to your negative keywords will decrease the chances that your ads will be shown to that audience. If a seller you're targeting as a keyword writes in multiple genres, you could enter the non-relevant subgenres and titles for that seller's product in your negative keyword list, so only readers searching for that product in your subgenre will be shown your ads. For instance, if you're targeting "iPhones" as keywords, you might want to add android as a negative keyword. You can specify either Negative Phrase or Negative Exact for match type, depending on how much you want to limit the likelihood of your ad being matched to a non-relevant product.

Testing keywords

The only way to test a keyword is to try it out! And if it performs well in one ad, check it in a second, and then the third one, until you're sure you have a winner. Also, don't expect keywords to behave the same in all ads. A keyword that generates a lot of clicks and sales in one ad might have to scratch and claw to get impressions in another. How well a keyword performs can be influenced by the bid amount, how effectively it pairs with the ad copy for the ad, how many other people are bidding at the time lots of things! But as your campaign history grows and you have more information to work with, you'll see trends for specific keywords.

You'll learn which ones to mark off your lists, which ones are steady producers, and which ones are shining stars. Adding keywords to existing campaigns, you can add keywords to a campaign until you hit the 1000 keyword limit. You'll find an "Add Keywords" button at the top of each of your campaign dashboards. Add a single keyword to a campaign, or copy and paste in a list of new keywords from a text document or spreadsheet. Set the Match and CPC (Cost Per Click) Bid price you want to apply to all the keywords you're adding and click the Add button.

Your new keywords will be added to the campaign. You'll find detailed information about setting Bids in the next chapter. More is not always better! This is another hotly contested topic when it comes to AMS ads. For each keyword ad, you're allowed up to 1000 keywords. That's a lot of words, and there are plenty of sellers who will tell you to hit as close to that number as you can with every ad. And that can work. However, you can also get great results with ads that contain only 150 keywords or less. Don't be afraid to start small and grow! You may find that you get better results from a short, targeted list than a large, amorphous one. I certainly do. And those 1000 keyword behemoths can quickly turn into dead weight if you don't do routine maintenance.

Chapter 7:

How to have the right mindset?

We will talk about what you should be doing, to make sure that you are not failing in your endeavors to start this Amazon FBA to live a healthier life overall.

This chapter will show you what you could be doing to make this Amazon FBA your lifestyle and to not only help you start the Amazon FBA and stay on track but also to live with this eating plan for the rest of your life.

These daily patterns will help you to not fail with your Amazon FBA, and we understand that you may fail a couple of times in any Amazon FBA, and it is understandable to do so.

Nonetheless, this chapter will show you how to make sure you are consistent and not failing.

These habits have been followed by many successful people, to get optimal results in all of their aspects of life, whether it be fitness related or anything else. Make sure you start implementing all of these habits after you are done reading this book as it will help you to make this Amazon FBA your lifestyle.

The reason why this chapter might sound philosophical is that the only way you will see success with this Amazon FBA is if you do it consistently. For you to do that, you need to change your current lifestyle by being more productive and disciplined. You have to remember, healthy eating is more than just an Amazon FBA. It's a lifestyle.

Plan your day ahead

Planning your day ahead of time is crucial, not only does planning out your day help you be more prepared for your day moving forward, but it will also help you to become more aware of the things you shouldn't be doing, hence wasting your time.

Moreover, planning your day will truly help you with making the most out of your time, that being said, we will talk about two things:

1. Benefits of planning out your day;
2. How to go about planning out your day.

So, without further ado, let us dive into the benefits of planning out your day.

Establishing priorities

Yes, planning out your day will help you prioritize a lot of things in your day to day life. You can allow time limits to the things you want to work on the most to least.

For example, if you're going to write your book and you are super serious about it, you need a specific time limit every day in which you work on a task wholeheartedly without any worries of other things until the time is up. Then you move on to the next job in line, so when you schedule out your whole day, and you give yourself time limits, then you can prioritize your entire day.

The same thing goes for your Amazon FBA, make sure you allocate time for prepping your plans for the next day, which will allow you to have goals ready for you when you need it hence making it easy for you to continue on with your Amazon FBA.

More focus on the task at hand

This point is quite similar to the previous point. Once you have started to plan out your day and you have become more aware of the things that you are about to do. With the time limit on all tasks that you do daily, it will create an urgency to get as much of the job done as you can before time is up and you are moving on to your next appointment. Which one will help you be more focused on the task at hand and get more things done? Many people consider planning your day out to be time-consuming, but it isn't if you prioritize your time the right way. If you plan your goals the day before, then it should not be a problem.

Work-life balance

You see, once you start planning out your whole day, you become more aware of your time and how to balance it out. Once you begin to write out your entire day ahead, you will know precisely what you are doing that day, so you don't have to do anything sporadically throughout the day.

Always plan some time for yourself every day where you can wind down by reading a good book, meditating or maybe hanging out with your friends. You will feel refreshed the next day, having to wind down and "chill out" will only make you a more productive person.

Planning out your whole day ahead will not only help you prioritize better. It will also help you be more focused on your task at hand and will help you have a better work-life balance. This also means that you are eating foods that you like once in a while. This will help you to stay motivated with the Amazon FBA that you are following. So now that we have covered the benefits of planning out your day, let's dive into the how to's when it comes to planning out your day.

Summarize your normal day

Now, before we start getting into planning out your whole day ahead, you need to realize that to plan your entire day, you need to know precisely what you are doing that day. That means you need to write down every single thing you do on a typical day and the time you start and end it. It needs to be detailed in terms of how long does it take for your transportation to get to work, etc.

Now, after you have figured out your whole day, you can decide how to prioritize your day. Moving on could be cutting out a task that you don't require or shortening your time for a job that doesn't need that much time. After you have your priorities for the day, you can add pleasurable tasks into your day like hanging out with your friends, etc.

Arrange your day

It is crucial that you arrange your day correctly, so the best way to organize your day is to make sure you get all your essential stuff done earlier in the day when your mind is fresh.

After that's done, you can have some time for yourself to relax and do whatever it is that you want. But make sure you get all the things that need to be done before you can move on to free time for yourself. Another thing that will help you is to set time limits on each task, and once you start setting time limits, you will be more likely to get the job done.

Remove all the fluff

So, what I mean by that is removing all the things that are holding you back from achieving your goals. Make sure you remove all of the things that are holding you back from getting the things that you need to be doing. If you have time for the fluff, do it, if not, then work on your priorities first.

In conclusion, planning out your day will help you tremendously! Make sure you plan out your day every day to ensure successful and accomplished days.

Be grateful

We will be talking about how to be grateful and what are the benefits of being thankful for what you have! Now believe it or not being grateful every day will help you Get more things done while keeping your mood elevated, see when your thankful for the things you have you will start to feel like your mind will be in peace and joy. When your mind is in order and comfort, you will be more productive with all the tasks ahead of you that day. Being in a grateful state of mind will help you become less stressed and more positive, which will help your work quality by ten folds. So, it is pretty essential that you stay grateful not only for better work performance but to also be in a peaceful state of mind. This will also help you to do more positive things with your Amazon FBA, such as eat healthy throughout the day. Let's discuss the three main benefits of being thankful.

Helps you start your day

Of course, if you start your day in a happy mood, you will more likely be keen to do more stuff and be more productive. If you read up on the most dedicated people and their day to day life, you will know that successful people tend to practice the same habits which I am going to be talking about in this chapter. The benefit of saying things you are grateful for first thing in the morning will boost your positive vibes when you talk about the things, you're thankful and you will complain and attract negative vibes a lot less! You always want to be in a positive mood as much as you can. To make sure you have a positive vibe, write or say things you are grateful towards.

You will become more approachable

Yes, being grateful will make you more approachable! Believe it or not, people do sense your "vibes" when you

124

walk into the door. When you're more thankful about life, you are happier and more positive, which is what people want to be around. Who knows, the next person you see could be an opportunity for you to grow your business or get a new job! So always make sure you are in a great mood and counting your blessings still as good things will come to you.

Lowered stress levels

I think this point is very self-explanatory. Let me ask you, what most people are stressed about? Lack of resources, plain and straightforward.

A lack of resources creates 99% of the stress. Once you start counting what you have rather than what you don't have, you begin to become a lot less stressed, which is more suitable for your physical and mental health! So, make sure you always stay in a grateful mood. If you want to understand more about how being grateful can change your life, I recommend reading "The Magic" by Rhonda Byrne.

So, all in all, being grateful will help you live a better life and be more successful. Now you might be wondering how to be thankful throughout the day since it is so hard to block out ungrateful thoughts, well I'll show you three techniques that will help you combat your ungrateful thoughts and keep you in a grateful "vibe" most of your life.

Write ten things you are grateful for every morning

You see, writing what you are thankful for will make your life a lot easier and help you start your day in gratitude. What I want you to do is: first, get a notebook/diary. Then, as soon as you wake up, I want you to write ten things you're grateful for. This could be anything from small such as having water to drink to have a nice car, the whole point of this is to make you start your day in gratitude since the way your entire day is going to be most of the time. So, make sure to start your day on the right foot by writing down ten things you're grateful for.

Don't forget the 1/5 ratio

This is something I came up with, and it works great for me. You see, whenever I say something I am angry or not grateful for, I always say five things I am super thankful for right after to get myself into the grateful "vibe". In the beginning, this method will be your best friend as it will save you from killing your "vibe".

Cut out negative people

This task might be the hardest to do, but it is quite essential, the people who you are around are the people who will create your personality.

If you are around negative people, you will develop adverse circumstances for yourself, so if you are around people who are not upbeat about life and find everything wrong and never see the good in anyone, you need to cut them out and be around people who are happy and ready for what life has to offer. Now I get it, some cynical people can be your family members, and you can't cut them out, the best thing to do is:

- Make them understand what they are doing wrong;
- Show them how they can change their life and if they still want to remain the same, then keep your distance.

In conclusion, it is essential that you are in a grateful "vibe" as it will not only help you with your mental and physical health, but it will also help you attract better people and better circumstances. Don't forget to practice the three methods we discussed in this chapter for you to be in a grateful "vibe" throughout the day and whole life! That being said I hope this chapter shed some light on the importance of being grateful and how it can make or break your life, and I hope you don't take this chapter lightly being grateful is the most critical thing you can do to turn your life around. So, be thankful!

Now that we have covered the part of being grateful, and how it can help you with your day to day life and eating habits. Let us give you some concrete ideas on how to change the way you live your experience and to make it better.

Stop multitasking

I think we are all guilty of this at a time, and if are multitasking right now, I need you to stop.

Now, multitasking could be a lot of things. It could be as small as cooking and texting at the same time, or it could be as big as working on two projects at the same time. Studies are showing how multitasking can reduce your quality of work, which something you don't want to do if your goal is to get the best result out of the thing that you are doing. That being said, there are a lot more reasons as to why you shouldn't be multitasking, so without further ado, lets dive into the primary reasons why multitasking can be harmful.

You're not as productive

Believe it or not, you tend to be a lot less productive when you are multitasking. When you go from one project to another or anything else for that matter, you don't put all your effort into your work. You are always worried about the project that you will be moving into next.

So, moving back and forth from one project to another will definitely affect your productivity if you want to get the most out of your work you need to be focused on one thing at a time and make sure you get it done to the best of your abilities. Plus, you are more likely to make mistakes, which will not help you work to the best of your ability.

You become slower at your work

When you are multitasking, chances are you will end up being slower at completing your projects. You would be in a better position if you were to focus on one project at a time instead of going back and forth, which of course helps you complete them faster.

So, the thing that enables you to be faster at your projects when you're not multitasking is the mindset, we often don't realize how much mindset comes into play.

When you are going back and forth from one project to another, you are in a different mental state going into another project which takes time to build and break. So, by the time you have managed to get into the mindset of project A you are already moving into project B, it is always best that you devote your time and energy one project at a time if you want it to doe did an at a faster pace.

Affects your creativity

This is a significant disadvantage of multitasking, and studies are showing that multitasking can negatively affect your creativity. When something requires too much focus from your end, it becomes harmful to your creativity, and you need a lot more attention when multitasking compared to working on one thing at a time. If you want to succeed and live a better life, then you need to be creative, so if multitasking affects your creativity, then you need to stop doing that.

By now, you can see how multitasking can hinder the ability for you to work at your best. Not only does multitasking help not be prolific but makes you slower and less creative.

So, all the benefits you thought you were getting multitasking was not accurate after all, nonetheless, by now, you might be wondering how to go about working most efficiently.

Well, the best way to put it is to work on one project at a time, I want you to put all your time and energy in the project you are doing currently and not worry about other projects. Make sure you set yourself goals when you start the project which will help you be more efficient and faster at your work, so an example would be "you will not move on to another project until project A has been completed" or you have managed to hit a certain threshold at that specific project. So, to sum it all up.

Set yourself a goal (time, quality, etc.)

All in all, multitasking will do you no good. It will only make you slower at your work and make you less productive. Making sure you stop multitasking is essential, as it will only help you live a better life.

One thing to remember from this chapter is to put all your energy at one thing at a time, and this will yield you a lot of better projects or anything that you are working towards to be great. If you want to be more successful and live a better life, you need to make sure your projects are quality as I can't stress this point enough.

You are probably reading this book because you want to get better at living your life or achieve goals that you just haven't yet.

One of the reasons why you are not living the life that you want or haven't reached your goal could be a lot of things but, one of the items could be the quality of your work. So, review yourself, and find out why you haven't achieved your goal and why you are not living the life that you want.

If you happen to stumble upon multitasking being the limiting factor or the quality of your work, I want you to stop and start working on one project at a time while giving it your full attention. What you will notice is that your work will have a higher quality and will be completed in a quicker amount of time following the steps listed above, which will change your life and help you achieve your life goals in a better more efficient way.

After reading this chapter, many might be thinking that this is more of a self-help book than it is an Amazon FBA book. The truth is that we want you to understand how to live a better life by changing the habits that you are currently following.

Truth be told, following an Amazon FBA business and making it a lifestyle is a lot more work than you think it is. For you to make it easy, you need to understand that you need to change your habits in order to be successful at this Amazon FBA business. Which means you need to change the way you move the way you think and the way you perform.

This chapter gives you a clear idea on how to start living a better life by changing up your habits. Once you do change your practices you will notice that following the Amazon FBA business as a whole will be very easy for you. The reason why it will be straightforward for you is that you will change the way you move and change the way you live your life in general.

Many people thinks that Amazon FBA business as not being a part of a lifestyle. But the truth is that they don't realize that it needs to be a lifestyle for it to be a health benefit. If you want to be healthier then you need to make sure that you're taking care of your health 24/7, 365 days a year.

Chapter 8:

Find the right product to launch

Finding the right product to sell on Amazon may not be the most straightforward task, considering selling something that you like may already be sold by others. After all, you are in this game for profit. To achieve your objectives, you may need to go the extra mile to discover the hidden secrets of selling on this global platform.

The ideal product to be sold on Amazon needs to have high demand associated with low competition to ensure that it isn't sold by many merchants. This is common sense since your goal is to find a niche that meets such a requirement. Having your private label can be a considerable advantage in this case, because you can mark your place in the market. You can then go after the potential customers without being bothered by competitors.

In this chapter, you can find all the necessary details related to products, which can get jaw-dropping high profits, how to conduct market research, how to test your competition, and which bestseller categories are on Amazon.

When hundreds of millions of products are being sold on this platform, choosing the right goods to advertise can prove to be a challenging task. That's why you have to know exactly what you are looking for in the Amazon catalog. By respecting the general guidelines, you can also find the best products to sell.

How to recognize a good product

What is the ideal product to sell on Amazon? How does it look like? What are the main characteristics you need to consider when choosing merchandise? These are only a few questions to ask yourself at the beginning of this process.

Regarding the latest question, you can find some key information on how to recognize the best product.

Affordable retail price

According to recent studies, a price range (usually between $25 and $50) is big enough to cover fees on Amazon related to storage, fulfillment, and advertising.

This is when you have high sales, and the volume of sales can easily cover all these expenses and guarantee a handsome profit. Generally, if the price is above $50, then many of the customers will no longer consider its attractiveness, and the rate of the goods is what people see. Hence, the purchases will drop significantly.

Very low seasonality

Meaning, the ideal outcome is not influenced by season fluctuation of sales. You need a product that can generate profits throughout the whole year, not just during a specific season.

Lesser reviews for the top sellers

Usually, 200 is a good value in this case. However, less than 100 would be even better.

Room for improvement

You can analyze the feedback received from the customers and improve your product based on them.

Easy manufacturing

Such a product has to be easily manufactured and made of resistant materials. Thus, you probably need to avoid glass. You also have to keep it simple. So, electronics and sophisticated goods are some examples of the things you should avoid. Of course, these are just guidelines since your ideal product may be different from the other merchants. It's all about knowing exactly what to sell in the niche you choose to conduct your business.

Finding products fast and easy

By this moment, you know what to look for in the massive database of the Amazon platform. However, you will need some proper tools to help you in this challenging mission. You need to find measurable information related to products, such as demand, price, seasonality, sales, rating, dimensions, price, and many more.

The Jungle Scout Web App can come in handy to help you scan the products from the platform using the Product Database extension.

Another exciting feature is the Product Tracker, which can enable you to track inventory, sales activity, rankings, and prices over some time. To make up your mind regarding the products to sell on Amazon, you need to track them for a few weeks before deciding after viewing the report provided by the Product Tracker feature. By doing so, you can get a clear idea about how the product performs.

If you want to find a suitable niche with high demand, a handy tool can be the Niche Hunter feature of the Jungle Scout Web App. This extension analyzes the most frequent keywords to discover in-demand goods. It can display a list with plenty of products that buyers search for as well.

Furthermore, the feature provides an Opportunity Score, which is based on a search algorithm called Listing Quality Score (LQS). It is responsible for identifying the products with high demand and extremely low listing. The higher the Opportunity Score is, the better. The

Jungle Scout Web App can also be used with the Google Chrome extension to test a multitude of keywords. This process can also display some impressive results from which you can easily find out the competition levels for many products. Using all these tools, you can come up with a list of 20 products that fit all of your requirements, but these products will have to be tested.

Comprehensive market research

Once you made up your mind regarding the products you want to sell, the first question you need to ask yourself is: "How many items can I sell during a month?". The goods which have to be filtered by this query have to respect the following two requirements:

- **Proper sales distribution**
  Meaning, one or two merchants do not dominate the niche market. Instead, the sales are distributed amongst a few sellers

- **Satisfactory demand**
  Satisfactory demand is considered when the most active sellers on this market can easily sell at least ten items per day. If you can generate ten sales

per day or 300 per month, that's an outstanding figure to start with on Amazon. Jungle Scout extension can help you with this research since it can easily display a report after typing a few relevant keywords. Aside from the top merchandisers, it will also inform you of their sales volume, product prices, item demand, and many more.

Test your competition

After you have shortlisted the products that you want to sell, the second question to ask is: "What is the competition selling this item for?".

Again, the Jungle Scout App can come in handy since it can show you some fascinating information like reviews and score ratings. The reviews are the most important aspect to think about when analyzing your competitors since the number can give you a distinct idea about the size of the competition. A high number of the review indicates a very competitive market: the kind of category you have to stay away from.

Moreover, the tool can also show you a list of products on demand that have a small number of reviews. This information is pure gold because that is what you need to get into.

Excellent opportunities are usually referred to as highly demanded products with less than 200 reviews. When we're talking about less than 100 studies, these are unique chances.

To do your homework properly when assessing competition, you may need to read its reviews to improve your products before selling them as well.

Furthermore, you can use the Jungle Scout app to establish which items will be your secondary products. These are the goods that you can still get some profits out of, but you may need to track the results for at least a week or two. By doing so, you are already one step ahead of your competitors. Also, when studying your competition, it matters to think about a significant feature: Amazon Best Seller Ranking.

To explain this term simply, it refers to the order of the products that are being listed on a page. The platform sorts and arranges every merchandise that was sold at least once into a hierarchy, which is the Best Seller Ranking (BSR).

Using this indicator and the Jungle Scout sales estimator tool you can roughly calculate the product sales volume of your competitors. To be specific, you can choose the category, the marketplace, enter the BSR, and obtain their sales estimation. Such a tool can provide you with the right information to become one step in front of your competition once you apply the proper strategies and get the expected results. If the items that you are selling only have a few reviews, you can seriously play a significant role in this market niche after making some sales. To be successful on Amazon, you will need to sell the right products. To make that happen, you have to be extremely practical and sell what is in high demand and has high chances to be sold. It does not necessarily have to be what you like because there may be plenty of other merchants desiring the same product.

Furthermore, you might face steep competition with more established sellers if you insist on doing so. You also have to be incredibly passionate about the products you are selling because you need to know everything about every merchandise to provide the information that the customers need to see, as well as to improve its quality. That is one way for you to create a well-appreciated brand, which the consumers will want to trust and buy from again.

Best Selling categories on Amazon

One good starting point to select the right products to sell on this platform is to check the statistics of the bestselling categories and sub-categories.

The good news is that it's the kind of information that can readily be found on the Amazon website. Therefore, you can browse through the site's categories and wait for each one to display the best sellers. If you limit your search on the specific sections, you will find the best-selling merchants, who may also be extremely competitive. That's why tackling them may not be the wisest thing to do.

However, if you go further and browse through the sub-categories, you may come across best sellers that are worth your efforts. Some products are merely better sold under a private brand, but the areas that may be for everyone are: kitchen and dining pet supplies sports and outdoor patio, lawn, and garden home and kitchen

Chapter 9:
Back end problems

Many people do not realize that signing up as an FBA seller on Amazon has implications for business and taxes. For this reason, you will most likely need to register your business to collect tax from the buyer on the items you sell and pass those taxes on to the state. Amazon works on a quarterly system, so you will need to collect your tax information every quarter.

Federal taxes

Your business constitutes a form of self-employment. For this reason, you will need to do the paperwork for the Self-Employment tax in order to pay for your income tax. You will also need to pay Medicare tax on your salaried income and Social Security taxes, though this depends on the income you make.

Collecting sales tax

The first thing you will need to do is register with the sales tax board of the state you are living in. Only after doing this can you begin to collect taxes on the items you sell. Otherwise, you will be collecting taxes illegally. If you are already a seller on Amazon, you will be familiar with the obligation to collect sales tax. However, while in many ways, Amazon FBA makes running your business easier in terms of tax collection, it becomes a little more complicated. This is because you are utilizing Amazon's distribution warehouses in multiple States. You are thus involved in multiple state tax nexuses. The legal situation surrounding nexuses is still in limbo. There are new developments happening all the time.

Because online businesses are so new, regulations regarding sales tax are still in their infancy and you will need to be vigilant about these issues to be sure you are in compliance with the most up-to-date versions of these laws.

There are only five States that do not collect sales tax in the U.S. Every other state has one form or another of the requirements about collecting sales tax. If your inventory is being stored in a State, you will need to collect sales tax on it. As an individual seller, this is pretty straightforward: you are shipping from your home state, and will need to register your business there and get a permit to collect sales tax there.

With FBA as a professional seller, it is not so straightforward. This means you need to find out where Amazon is storing your inventory. Once you find out where the merchandise has been stored, then you can go about registering for permits to collect sales tax on the items you have sold.

Since you are running a small business, there are tax tips for calculating your overall spending. When buying items through retail arbitrage, save the receipts.

Be sure to record the mileage of your trips to the store as business expenses. It is advisable to get into contact with a tax accountant to avoid running into legal issues once your business becomes profitable.

This guide will help with the basic outlines of the action you can take with regard to initial awareness of tax issues, but it is not comprehensive.

Where should I be collecting sales tax?

You will find this information in your Amazon reports. Access your Reports on the Seller Central page.

Under the Inventory tab, click on "Inventory Event Detail" and download the report. Once you have loaded the report into Excel (or whatever spreadsheet reading software you choose to use), you have to find the specific column that tells you where your items have been shipped. Use the filter tool to look up the column with the name fulfillment-cent-id. This is the name used in Amazon reports to show where your goods have been stored. It consists of a three-letter code followed by either a 1, 2, or 3. The letters indicate the code for the airport closest to the distribution center. So the airport is usually located in the State of the distribution center. By looking up the airport codes listed in your Amazon report to find out what State they are located in, and comparing those airport codes to the locations of Amazon Fulfillment centers, you should be able to tell which states your items have been stored in. There are also services available that will find this type of information for you if you are inclined to outsource this work.

How do I collect taxes in the States I have a sales nexus in?

Once you have established the locations of the States where your goods have been stored, you will likely need to apply for a sales tax permit or license for that state. Each state has different requirements for registering for a sales tax permit. You will need to apply and register for every state your items are stored in.

Most States do not charge a fee for registering as a business and collecting sales tax, which is not to say that all of them don't. There are five States that do not require any registration.

You can pay for a service that will establish your tax needs for you and take care of the rest. There are other websites with guides on the requirements for registering in every state that also offer services for handling your taxes through Amazon, however, it is wise to consult a lawyer to avoid making mistakes and risk auditing.

Amazon also offers its own services for Professional Sellers.

By clicking on the "Settings" section of Seller Central, you can select "Tax Settings" and begin setting up Amazon's tax collection services. Amazon charges for its tax collection services, but it may be worth the charge in light of the extensive complications brought up in dealing with so many tax nexuses. With Amazon's service, you are required to calculate the refunds yourself.

Conclusion

As you can see, we learned a lot in this book. Not only did we teach you how to build an Amazon FBA business, but we also showed you how to do it properly.

Make sure that you read this book thoroughly before you make any decisions on your transaction, as we have given you all the tools you need to be successful in the long term. That being said, if you're a beginner, then this book is ideal for you as it gives you the step by step process on Amazon FBA. We talked about many things that most people don't talk about, which is what makes our books so much better than others.

Moreover, we spoke about how to pick out the right product appropriately without spending a lot of time, and this is very important to do when starting an Amazon FBA business. Unlike Shopify, you don't have to worry about building a brand so much. Also, it makes it very easy for you to start making money on Amazon FBA since Amazon already gets a lot of visitors.

That being said, thank you so much for reading this box of the end, and we hope you learned a lot from it.

150